*Culinary Arts Institute®*

# FOOD PROCESSOR COOKBOOK

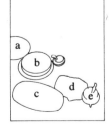

# FOOD PROCESSOR COOKBOOK

FOOD PROCESSOR COOKBOOK

**Linda Carter: Contributing Editor**
**and the Culinary Arts Institute Staff**

Edward Finnegan: Executive Editor

Book designed and coordinated by Charles Bozett

Illustrations by Diana Magnuson

Cover photo: Bob Scott Studios     Inside Photos: Zdenek Pivecka

Adventures in Cooking SERIES

Culinary Arts Institute
A DIVISION OF DELAIR/CONSOLIDATED    new york

ISBN: 0-8326-0607-3

# INTRODUCTION

It has been said of the food processor: "It is not a machine; it is a phenomenon." Certainly, it is the cooking sensation sweeping the country. It is the first major breakthrough in kitchen appliances since the blender, which was the first breakthrough since the mixer. The extraordinary feature of the food processor is that it can almost replace both these machines.

*What exactly is a food processor?* What does it do? What makes it such an exciting and unique invention? The food processor is a multipurpose machine combining the functions of several appliances. It is a mixer, blender, meat grinder, food mill, ice crusher, peanut butter maker, dough kneader, grater, slicer, chopper, and shredder, all in one. It performs more chores better and faster than any other kitchen helper—including the live-in chef! In a matter of seconds, it chops vegetables to any desired consistency, processing hard vegetables like carrots, turnips, and potatoes as efficiently as softer vegetables like mushrooms, onions, and parsley. It chops meat into a hamburgerlike consistency at the rate of one pound per minute. It makes a "perfect every time" pastry dough in less than forty-five seconds. It mixes and kneads a one-pound loaf of bread in less than two minutes. It chops ice. It grates Parmesan and other hard cheeses into a fine powder. It makes bread crumbs. It chops nuts and even makes nut butters. It purées cooked vegetables and fruits for sauces and soups. It makes sausages, patés, stuffings, mincemeat, and mousse. It makes dips, flavored butters, cakes, mayonnaise, and pasta. In addition, it slices at the rate of one pound per minute: round slices, long slices, thick slices, thin slices, and even diagonal slices. It shreds vegetables, soft cheeses, and meats into long or short shreds, shredding a head of cabbage in thirty seconds. It also processes delicate julienne strips, or matchstick and shoestring shapes. The capabilities of the food processor go on and on and are as varied as the imagination.

The food processor industry began in this country about 1973 with the introduction of the Cuisinart™ Food Processor, a French import. The phenomenal success of this machine generated a wave of interest and enthusiasm among professionals in the world of cooking, and as a result, numerous magazine and newspaper articles appeared extolling the virtues of the Cuisinart™ Food Processor. A New York food columnist ranked its invention with such things as "the printing press, the cotton gin, the steamboat, paper clips, and contour sheets." One well-known cookbook author refers to it as "a robot in the kitchen," claiming that "anyone who loves to cook will wonder how he or she ever lived without it. I know I couldn't." Another well-known cookbook author is an avid fan of the food processor, and uses it in many of her recipes, referring to it as "the super-blender-food processor."

Consumer response has been equally enthusiastic. As a result, a number of American manufacturers have been inspired to develop similar food processors. There are also other units, not called food processors, that have numerous attachments and accomplish most of the same functions. These include the Oster Kitchen Center, the Kenwood Chef, the KitchenAid Mixer, the Bosch Food Mixer, the Braun Kitchen Machine, and the Starmix. It is interesting to note that many of these machines have been available for years, but it has taken the wave of interest generated by the Cuisinart™ Food Processor to alert consumers to the usefulness of multipurpose food-processing machines.

Just as there is a wide variety of food processors, there is also a wide range of performance standards and price tags. Any food processor is a substantial kitchen investment, ranging in price from $70 to $225. In most cases, the performance level rises with the price. As all food processors perform a wide range of functions, there is a food processor to meet everyone's culinary needs and budget.

If you are considering buying a food processor, carefully compare the various machines and consider which one best fulfills your cooking requirements. Because the food processor is such a unique and magically fast machine, it has to be seen in action to be believed. Many stores offer food processor demonstrations for this purpose which are helpful and informative. Familiarize yourself with the literature provided with each machine, and become aware of the advantages and limitations of each. Whichever your choice, you can be assured of gaining the assistance of a "robot in the kitchen." Adapt the food processor to your style of cooking, let it work for you, and you will discover a new, exciting world of culinary delights.

# CONTENTS

# ETHNIC DINNER MENUS

## ORIENTAL DINNER

*Egg Rolls (page 22)*
*Shrimp Dumplings in Chicken Broth (page 24)*
*Sweet and Sour Chicken (page 37)*
*Beef with Pea Pods and Water Chestnuts (page 34)*
*Pork Fried Rice (page 64)*
*Almond Cookies (page 89)*

## JEWISH DINNER

*Chopped Chicken Livers (page 16)*
*Gefilte Fish (page 17)*
*Stuffed Cabbage (page 46)*
*Beef Brisket (page 33)*
*Mushroom Kugel (page 58)*
*Sweet Potato Tzimmes (page 62)*
*Upside-down Passover Prune Cake (page 84)*

## MEXICAN DINNER

*Guacamole (page 16)*
*Gazpacho (page 30)*
*Mexican Picadillo with Rice (page 34)*
*Green Chili Cornbread (page 81)*
*Mexican Christmas Eve Salad (page 69)*
*Mexican Peach Pastries (page 92)*

## GREEK DINNER

*Feta Cheese Strudel (page 46)*
*Moussaka (page 42)*
*Greek-Style Carrots and Green Beans (page 57)*
*Rice Pilaf (page 63)*
*Greek Salad (page 67)*
*Greek Sesame Bread (page 77)*
*Honey Cheese Pie (page 87)*

## RUSSIAN DINNER

*Eggplant Caviar (page 17)*
*Cranberry-Beet Borscht (page 25)*
*Russian Salmon Mound (page 44)*
*Braised Cucumbers (page 57)*
*Russian Black Bread (page 76)*
*Russian Fruit and Nut Pudding (page 93)*

## ITALIAN DINNER

*Eggs in Parsley Sauce (page 16)*
*Escarole Soup with Tiny Meatballs (page 24)*
*Cheese Ravioli with Tomato Sauce (page 38)*
*Stuffed Zucchini (page 62)*
*Italian Bread (page 74)*
*Chocolate-Ricotta Cheese Cake (page 85)*

## GERMAN DINNER

*Caraway Cheese Twists (page 18)*
*Greens Soup (page 25)*
*Beef Rouladen with Spätzle (page 32)*
*Bavarian Carrots (page 57)*
*Spinach Salad with Hot Sweet and Sour Dressing (page 66)*
*Walnut Torte (page 70)*

## FRENCH DINNER

*Broccoli Roll with Mushroom Filling (page 52)*
*Cream of Carrot Soup (page 26)*
*Lamb Leg on a Bed of Spinach (page 40)*
*Baked Herb Potato Pancake (page 60)*
*Green Salad Vinaigrette (page 66)*
*Raspberry Mousse (page 92)*

# BASIC FOOD PROCESSOR TECHNIQUES

The food processor is an extremely versatile machine, capable of performing a wide range of functions. The beauty of the appliance is that it is a small, compact unit which is easy to use, clean, and care for. Most food processors consist of a base housing the motor, a bowl, a lid with feed tube and pusher, and four simple attachments: steel blade, plastic blade, shredding disc, and slicing disc.

The food processor can be an invaluable tool in the kitchen, as it reduces the tedious chores of food preparation to a matter of seconds. Because it is such a powerful and magically fast machine, it is easy for the novice to overprocess some foods. Following are simple descriptions of the basic procedures and techniques to help the beginner master the art of the food processor.

## THE STEEL BLADE

The steel blade is the most versatile and most frequently used attachment. It accomplishes the tasks of chopping, grating, mixing, blending, puréeing, and kneading. The results obtained depend on the technique used and the amount of time the food is processed. There are three basic procedures to follow when chopping with the steel blade:

1. *The on/off technique* is the first and most important basic procedure. The machine is turned on, then off, with a quick twist of the wrist—as quickly as you can say "on/off." This technique is important for two reasons: First, the steel blade spins at several hundred revolutions per minute, some as fast as 1,800 revolutions per minute. The on/off motion is a way to slow down the speed of the blade, thus allowing for more control in processing. Second, as the machine is turned on and off in such rapid succession, the food falls in towards the center of the bowl, thus preventing

any particles of food from spinning around the edge.

The importance of this technique cannot be overstressed. It should be used for any ingredients being chopped, as it is easier to control the consistency without the risk of overprocessing. Be sure to check the consistency of the contents of the bowl after each on/off motion and proceed in this manner until the desired texture is reached. If the machine is new, the lid sometimes fits so tightly that it is difficult to inspect the bowl. In this case, rub a little salad oil around the outside rim of the lid and the inside rim of the bowl.

2. *The cutting of ingredients into one-inch pieces* is the second basic procedure. Always remember that the food processor cannot do everything. Don't expect it to chop half a green pepper uniformly all by itself. The ingredients must be cut into small enough pieces first by hand. Let the food processor handle the more tedious aspect of food preparation.

3. *The processing of small quantities of food at a time* is the third basic procedure, especially important if a coarse consistency is desired, since it is easier to control and obtain a more uniform texture when processing a small quantity at a time. The food processor processes food so quickly that the fact that you have to do a number of small batches of food instead of just one is not really significant.

Note some specific examples.

*To chop parsley.* Trim parsley of all tough stems. Wash and dry thoroughly before processing. A salad spinner is an excellent way to dry parsley. Process desired amount of parsley, either a few sprigs or an entire bunch at a time, using quick on/off motions, until desired consistency is reached. (Note: Recipes in this cookbook call for fresh parsley, cleaned, trimmed, and *tightly* packed. As a general rule, the amount of chopped parsley will equal half of the measurement given. Thus, one cup of fresh parsley, cleaned, trimmed, and tightly packed, will yield one-half cup chopped.)

*To chop onions.* Peel and quarter the onions. If the onion is very large, cut it into smaller pieces than quarters. As a general rule, process no more than two onions at a time, always using quick on/off motions until desired consistency is reached. Remember, if a coarse chop is desired, process a small quantity at a time.

*To chop green peppers.* Trim and core the peppers and cut them into one-inch pieces. Process a small quantity (no more than one pepper at a time), using quick on/off motions. Because green peppers are such a watery vegetable, if a fine consistency is desired, it is better to process with the slicing disc first, then process the slices with the steel blade to obtain a finer consistency.

*To chop green onions.* Trim tops and bottoms of the onions. Cut whole green onions into one-inch pieces. Process, using quick on/off motions, until desired consistency is reached. If processing a small quantity, it is necessary to stop the machine occasionally, scrape down the green onions from around the edge of the bowl, and continue processing.

*To chop mushrooms.* Trim, rinse, and thoroughly dry the mushrooms. Process small quantities, using quick on/off motions, until desired consistency is reached. Always remove chopped mushrooms before adding more. Immediately sprinkle with lemon juice to prevent discoloring.

*To chop apples.* Pare, core, and quarter apples. If apples are large, cut into pieces smaller than quarters. Process small quantities, using quick on/off motions, until desired consistency is reached. Immediately sprinkle with lemon juice to prevent discoloring.

*To chop cucumbers.* Pare the cucumber and cut in half lengthwise. Remove the seeds (to reduce the liquid), wipe dry with paper towels, and cut into one-inch pieces. Process, using quick on/off motions, until desired consistency is reached. Hint: For a more uniform fine chop, shred cucumber first and then process with steel blade.

*To chop or grate carrots.* Pare the carrots, and cut into one-inch pieces. For a coarse chop, process a small quantity (one or two carrots at a time), using quick on/off motions. For a fine chop or a grated consistency, a large quantity can be processed (six to eight carrots at a time), simply by letting the machine run until a very fine consistency is obtained. Hint: If a piece of carrot has wedged itself between the blade and the side of the bowl, use the quick on/off technique a few times. If this does not dislodge it, stop the machine and remove the wedged piece of carrot. Empty the contents of the bowl and return the steel blade. Always make sure that the steel blade is down on the shaft as far as it can go before resuming use of the machine. Add carrots and continue processing to desired consistency.

*To chop or grate potatoes.* Follow the same instructions as for carrots. After grating, place grated potatoes in a colander to drain off excess water, if desired. Remember that the steel blade will not produce an even dice or cube, so for some soups and chowders, such dicing will have to be done by hand.

*To mince garlic.* Peel garlic. To process one clove of garlic, start the machine and drop the garlic clove through the feed tube and process for a few seconds. Using a spatula, scrape around sides of bowl to collect the finely minced garlic.

*To grate cheese.* To process hard cheeses like Parmesan or Romano to a fine powder, cut the cheese into one-inch cubes. Start the machine and drop the cubes of cheese, one at a time, through the feed tube at one-second intervals. Process to desired consistency.

*To chop ice.* Start the machine and drop the ice cubes, one at a time, through the feed tube. Process no more than four at one time. Process, using on/off technique, until desired texture is obtained.

*To chop raw meat.* Trim meat of gristle and excess fat. Cut meat into one-inch cubes. Process no more than one-half pound of meat at a time. As meat takes such a short amount of time to process, it is difficult to control the texture with a large quantity in the bowl. Process the meat for five seconds, then stop and check the consistency. Continue to process, using quick on/off motions, until desired consistency is reached. Hint: Processing pieces of fat with the meat often yields coarse chunks of fat. To eliminate this, cut off pieces of fat first and process them separately until finely chopped. Add desired amount of chopped fat to bowl when processing cubes of meat.

*To chop cooked meat or poultry.* For making salads, such as beef or chicken, cut meat into one-inch cubes. Process, using quick on/off motions, until desired consistency is reached. Remember that a wide range of consistencies is achievable, from a coarse and chunky salad to a patélike spread, depending upon the length of time processed.

*To chop nuts.* For coarsely chopped nuts, process a small amount (one-half cup) at a time, using quick on/off motions, until desired consistency is reached. For a fine dry chop, add some of the flour and/or sugar from the recipe to the bowl when processing the nuts. This helps to absorb some of the oil. For a fine dry nut powder to be used in tortes, process the nuts with the shredding disc first, then process with the steel blade, adding a little flour and/or sugar, and process, using quick on/off motions, to a fine powder.

*To make peanut butter.* Add shelled peanuts to the bowl, up to sixteen ounces at a time; the larger the quantity, the longer the processing time. Simply let the machine run for three to four minutes or longer until the consistency is creamy and smooth. If a chunky texture is desired, add a handful or so of whole peanuts when the peanut butter first becomes smooth. Process several seconds longer for a smooth, creamy base with chunks of peanuts throughout. Hints: If dry roasted peanuts are used, a tablespoon of peanut oil or honey may need to be added. For an interesting variation, add cashews instead of peanuts for a chunky consistency. Or, try processing peanuts and chocolate chips together to get a delicious chocolate-peanut butter spread. Or, add one or two ripe bananas to an already smooth peanut butter to get a fluffy banana-peanut butter spread.

*To make pastry dough.* All types of pastry dough can be made in the food processor. Follow the same procedure as is used for this standard pie crust. Add flour, salt, sugar, and shortening to the bowl. If the recipe calls for butter, use *frozen* butter, cut into one-inch pieces. Process dry ingredients and shortening together until shortening is cut into flour to desired fineness (usually ten or fifteen seconds). With machine on, add liquid ingredients through the feed tube and process until dough forms a ball (usually twenty or thirty seconds). Once this occurs, immediately remove from the bowl. Hint: When frozen butter is used, the dough is already chilled and can be rolled out immediately.

*To make bread dough.* There are probably as many methods for making bread in the food processor as there are owners. The method presented in this book has proved to be successful and particularly helpful in adapting standard bread recipes to the food processor. There are a few important procedures to follow. Due to the limited capacity of the bowl, only one loaf can be made at a time, three cups of flour being the maximum amount of flour the processor can handle. Any recipe calling for six cups of flour or less can be adapted to make two loaves. To do this, mix all of the ingredients *except* the flour in a one-quart measuring cup— yeast and water mixture, scalded milk or lukewarm water, butter, salt, sugar, shortening, etc.— and thoroughly mix together. In a separate container, measure half of the flour; if recipe calls for six cups of flour, measure three cups. Add two of the three cups of flour to the bowl. With the machine on, add half of the liquid ingredients through the feed tube and process for a few seconds until blended together. Add the remaining cup of flour, one-quarter cup at a time, until the dough forms into a smooth yet slightly sticky ball. Depending upon climatic conditions, varying amounts of flour may be needed, so never add all of the flour at once. It is important to point out that a dough with a certain proportion of flour to liquid has a tendency to get stuck around the blade and slow down, almost stop, the motor. If this occurs or sounds like it is going to occur, immediately stop the machine, clear away the dough from the blade with the spatula, and add about one-quarter cup more flour to the bowl. Start the machine and the dough should form itself into a ball and start spinning around the bowl. Once this occurs, let the ball of dough spin around the bowl for twenty or thirty seconds. This is the kneading process. Proceed with the bread dough in the usual manner. If bread requires a second kneading, that is done by hand. Repeat the process for the second loaf.

*To make cakes.* Cakes can be made successfully in the food processor, though careful attention must be paid so that they are not overprocessed. Due to the limited capacity of the bowl, not all cake recipes are suited to the food processor. To prepare a small cake recipe in the food processor, cream shortening, gradually add sugar, then eggs, flavorings, and liquids. Mix dry ingredients together and add all at once. Process very briefly (five or ten seconds), only until flour is incorporated into mixture. Do not overmix at this point! Cakes come out best when dry ingredients are added last, in this manner. The food processor does not adequately beat egg whites or whip cream, so a mixer is still needed for these two functions.

*To purée.* Process cooked ingredients for sauces and soups to desired consistency. When making a cream soup or gravy, strain ingredients to be puréed, reserving stock in pan. Process strained ingredients separately. Add a small amount of the liquid through the feed tube, then turn puréed mixture into stock in pan.

*To make butter* (one quarter pound). Place the blade and bowl in freezer to chill. Pour one cup whipping cream (preferably at least several days old) into chilled bowl and process two to three minutes, or until butter is formed. Turn mixture into a sieve to remove buttermilk; reserve the buttermilk for cooking or drinking. If desired, add salt or herbs to butter and blend. Remove butter from bowl and pack into desired container. Cover and chill thoroughly to harden.

## THE SLICING DISC

The slicing disc is the attachment used for all slicing chores. It is used to slice soft, delicate foods, such as strawberries, mushrooms, and bananas, as well as harder foods, such as carrots, potatoes, and turnips. All ingredients to be sliced must be fed through the feed tube, and therefore must be cut to fit the feed tube. They are pushed

down the feed tube with the pusher, *never* with hands or fingers. There are a few basic procedures to be followed when using the slicing disc.

1. Trim all ingredients to fit the feed tube. Most food processor owners buy ingredients as near as possible to the shape and size needed. There is such a thing as a food-processor carrot! The size of the feed tube on most machines is approximately four inches high by three inches wide, and is shaped to meet government safety regulations. If foods are to be sliced in a vertical position, cut into 3½-inch pieces. If they are to be sliced in a horizontal position, cut into 2½-inch pieces.

2. Trim all ingredients being sliced in a vertical position so that tops and bottoms are perfectly flat. This technique produces a more uniform slice and in many cases prevents the piece of food from turning over on its side.

3. The pressure that needs to be exerted on the pusher varies with the food being processed. Generally, the harder the ingredients the firmer the pressure. Never at any point should the food be jammed down through the feed tube.

Following are some specific instructions for slicing.

*To slice long round vegetables.* Use vegetables such as carrots, zucchini, cucumber, etc.; pare as needed. To slice vertically to yield round slices,

cut vegetable into 3½-inch lengths. Trim the top and bottom so that they are flat. Place upright in the feed tube, fitting in as many pieces as possible, and slice. To slice horizontally, cut the vegetable into 2½-inch lengths, place lengths horizontally in the feed tube, and slice. Hint: If slicing one piece of a round, narrow food, such as a piece of

zucchini which does not fill the feed tube, place that piece of food in the far side of the feed tube, right up against the side, so that the motion of the blade does not turn the food over but forces it against the side of the feed tube. Also, large fat carrots are easier to process than many skinny carrots. Large fat carrots sliced horizontally make excellent slices to be used for dips.

*To slice onions.* Peel onions. If too large to fit into the feed tube, cut in half lengthwise. Cut a thin

slice off the top and bottom so that it is flat. Slice one half at a time with firm pressure.

*To slice mushrooms.* Clean, trim, and thoroughly dry mushrooms. Place mushrooms horizontally

stem to stem in the feed tube, filling the feed tube almost full. Slice, using gentle pressure. Remember that not all slices will be perfect slices, just as not all slices done by hand are perfect slices.

*To slice cabbage for cole slaw.* Cut the head of cabbage in lengthwise quarters. If it is a large head, cut quarters in half again. Trim out hard core. Cut a thin slice off the top and bottom of

each cabbage wedge so that it is flat. This step makes the wedge of cabbage go down the feed tube perfectly straight, thus preventing it from turning over on its side, and eliminating those large, uneven pieces of cabbage.

*To slice green peppers.* Buy the narrowest green peppers possible. Cut a thin slice off the top and bottom of the pepper. Carefully remove core. Gently squeeze the whole pepper to fit into the feed tube. If it does not fit, make a lengthwise slice down one side of the pepper. Gently force the pepper into the feed tube. Slice, using gentle pressure.

*To slice lemons.* Buy the smallest, narrowest lemons possible. Roll lemon back and forth on the counter a few times, pressing hard to soften it. Cut a thin slice off the top and bottom. Squeeze the lemon to fit into the feed tube. Hint: The opening at the base of the feed tube is slightly larger than at the top of the feed tube. If the lemon will not fit down the top of the feed tube, try inserting it up through the bottom. Position the lemon so that it sits flat on the slicing disc. Slice, using firm pressure.

*To cut green beans french style.* Clean and trim fresh green beans and cut into 2½-inch lengths. Place the green beans horizontally in the feed tube, filling the feed tube almost full, and slice, using firm pressure.

*To slice raw meats.* The food processor is an invaluable tool in preparing foods for Oriental cooking, especially meats. To slice raw meat, it must be partially frozen. The best way to do this is to first cut the meat into blocks to fit the feed tube. Then, freeze the meat for one to two hours so that it is only *partially* frozen. There should be ice crystals in the meat and it should be possible to pierce it with a sharp knife. The meat should be very firm, but not frozen. Slice, using firm pressure.

*To slice cooked meat.* Meat such as ham, sausage, or pepperoni should be cold, but not frozen. Cut the meat to fit the feed tube and slice, using firm pressure.

*To cut julienne strips.* The slicing disc is also used to process foods into delicate julienne, matchstick, and shoestring shapes. There are two steps involved that, practiced a few times, are very easy to accomplish. First, cut the ingredient to be

processed into 2½-inch lengths. Place it horizontally in the feed tube and slice. Remove the slicing disc and the slices from the bowl. Reinsert the slicing disc. Holding the lid on its side with the pusher inserted, raise the pusher about one inch and pack the slices up through the bottom of the feed tube, forcing them up against the pusher. Pack as many slices as possible into the feed tube, wedging them in so that when the lid is turned right side up they will not fall out. Return the lid to the bowl and slice again. Repeat the procedure until all ingredients have been double sliced. This process works well with potatoes, sweet potatoes, zucchini, cucumbers, carrots (fat carrots!), turnips, salami, ham, firm cheeses, and slightly frozen softer cheeses.

*To julienne mushrooms.* Buy medium-size mushrooms. Wash and dry mushrooms and remove stems. Place mushroom cap flat side down in feed tube. Slice one at a time. This will yield round mushroom slices. Next, pack round slices up through the bottom of the feed tube, as described above. Slice again, using light pressure.

*To slice celery and green onions.* These are the only two ingredients fed through the feed tube with your fingers. To slice celery, hold untrimmed celery by the bottom of the stalk. Hold the piece of celery up against the right side of the feed tube. Start the machine and push the stalk of celery down the feed tube until fingers are at least two inches above the blade. Obviously the whole piece of celery cannot be sliced. To slice green onions, trim the onion. Holding the green onion at the top of the stalk, start the machine and run the onion down the right side of the feed tube. Stop when fingers are two inches above the blade.

## THE SHREDDING DISC

The shredding disc is the attachment used to process ingredients into shredlike pieces of food, the size of the shred depending upon the position of the food in the feed tube. To produce long, delicate shreds, almost like a fine julienne, cut the ingredient into 2¹/₂-inch lengths and place them horizontally in the feed tube. This is an excellent process for carrots when making a carrot salad, or for cheese when making a pizza topping. Remember to use light pressure when shredding cheese. To make cole slaw of a finer consistency than is achieved with the slicing disc, use the shredding disc.

The shredding disc adds a new dimension to salad making. To give salads a different flavor, shred a variety of vegetables not ordinarily used, such as turnips, rutabagas, radishes, or zucchini. Either sprinkle them over the top or toss them in with the salad, or simply have fun experimenting with new combinations of salad materials, new shapes, and new textures.

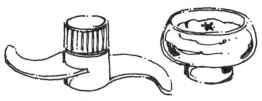

## THE PLASTIC BLADE

Though the plastic blade is the least-used attachment, there are several specific uses for which it is indispensable. It is basically used for processing ingredients of a lighter consistency, such as salad dressings, mayonnaise, sauces, light batters, frostings, omelets, and some dips and spreads. It is particularly useful for blending ingredients together, as it mixes without necessarily processing finer.

For example, use the plastic blade when making egg salad, tuna salad, or chopped liver, as it produces a coarser texture. (If a patélike consistency is desired, use the steel blade.) Or, use the plastic blade when mixing meat mixtures, such as meat loaf or meatballs. After all the ingredients have been separately processed, use the plastic blade to blend them together.

## HELPFUL HINTS

• When trimming foods to fit the feed tube, save the leftover scraps, storing them in a plastic bag in the refrigerator. For your next sauce or stew, cook them and process with the steel blade until puréed.

Use this puréed mixture as a thickening agent, as it cuts down on calories but adds nutrition and flavor.

• In a similar manner, cook all roasts on a bed of finely chopped vegetables, such as carrot, celery, onion, etc., with a little stock or wine added, if desired. For gravy, strain vegetables, process with steel blade until puréed, and add to gravy. Again, it adds body and flavor.

• The next time a creamed soup curdles, process it in small batches with the steel blade and watch the curdles disappear!

• Carefully consider the size and shape of ingredients processed through the feed tube. This will eliminate unnecessary trimming and waste.

• When adapting your own recipes to the food processor, consider the processing order of ingredients so as to minimize the washing of the bowl. Process dry ingredients first, such as bread crumbs, grated cheese, parsley, etc.

• One of the beauties of the food processor is that it processes small quantities of food at a time. A leftover portion of meat can be turned into an exciting sandwich spread. Or, with the addition of some cooked vegetables, the meat can be turned into baby food. Process with the steel blade to desired consistency.

• Do not use the rim of the bowl to clean off the spatula. Keep the rim free of food so that the lid can be turned smoothly and easily.

• Remember that the quality of the results obtained depends upon the quality of the ingredients used—firm, fresh vegetables are processed much more successfully than old, soft ones!

## SAFETY RULES

• *Most important rule of all:* Always wait for the blade or disc to come to a *complete stop* before removing the lid.

• Handle the steel blade and discs carefully—they are very sharp.

• When using the discs, always use the pusher to guide the food down the feed tube. Never use your fingers.

• Always make sure the blade or disc is firmly in the base of the bowl before starting the machine.

• Store the attachments in a safe place, out of reach of children.

**Note: All recipes in this cookbook were tested on the Cuisinart™ Food Processor. Other machines may have varying processing times.**

# APPETIZERS

# Eggs in Parsley Sauce

8  hard-cooked eggs
1  small clove garlic
2  cups fresh parsley, cleaned and trimmed (1 cup chopped)
1  small boiled potato, chilled
6  tablespoons lemon juice
¼  cup olive oil
½  cup vegetable oil
2  tablespoons capers or 1 small dill pickle
2  anchovy fillets
⅛  teaspoon pepper

1. Cut hard-cooked eggs in half lengthwise and place cut side down in a shallow serving dish.
2. Using **steel blade,** mince garlic. Add parsley and process until chopped. Add remaining ingredients and process until creamy and thoroughly blended.
3. Pour over eggs and serve.

*8 servings*

*Note:* This herb sauce is excellent served with hot or cold meats, or it makes a very tasty salad dressing.

# Chopped Chicken Livers

1  pound chicken livers
3  medium onions, peeled and quartered
3  tablespoons chicken fat
3  hard-cooked eggs
½  teaspoon salt
⅛  teaspoon pepper

1. Wash and trim livers.
2. Using **steel blade,** process onions, with quick on/off motions, until chopped.
3. Sauté onion in chicken fat until golden. Add livers and continue to cook until no longer pink inside (10 to 15 minutes).
4. Using **plastic blade,** add livers and onion, 2 of the hard-cooked eggs, salt, and pepper to bowl and process to desired consistency. (For a smooth patélike consistency, use **steel blade.**) You may need to add additional chicken fat.
5. Chill in refrigerator for at least 2 hours. Serve garnished with **finely chopped hard-cooked egg yolk** and **fresh parsley.**

# Guacamole

1  small clove garlic
2  large ripe avocados, peeled
2  tablespoons lemon juice
1  teaspoon chili powder (optional)
   Salt to taste

1. Using **steel blade,** mince garlic. Add avocado and remaining ingredients and process to desired consistency. (Remember to use quick on/off motions if a coarse, chunky consistency is desired.)
2. Serve as a dip with tortilla chips, on lettuce as a salad, or as a filling for tacos.

*About 2 cups dip*

*Note:* If not served immediately, refrigerate in a covered bowl with avocado pits immersed in guacamole. This will help prevent the avocado from darkening on standing.

**From the Oriental dinner menu on page 8:**
**Egg Rolls, 22, and Sweet and Sour Chicken, 37**

# Gefilte Fish

3 pounds fresh fish (whitefish, carp, and/or pike)
2 quarts water
2 teaspoons salt
½ teaspoon pepper
8 carrots, pared
4 medium onions, peeled and cut to fit feed tube
2 eggs
6 tablespoons ice water
4 tablespoons matzoh meal
2 teaspoons salt
½ teaspoon pepper

Horseradish

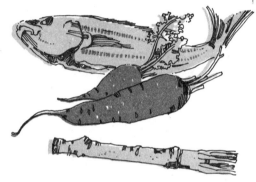

1. Have fish filleted, reserving head, bones, and skin.
2. In a large pot, place water, 2 teaspoons salt, ½ teaspoon pepper, 7 carrots, head, bones, and skin of fish.
3. Using **slicing disc,** slice 3½ onions (cut remaining ½ onion in half and reserve). Add sliced onion to the pot, bring to a boil, lower heat, and simmer while fish is being prepared.
4. Cut fish into 2-inch pieces. Using **steel blade,** process fish in 1-pound batches to pastelike consistency. Remove to a large bowl and repeat 2 more times with remaining fish. After all fish has been processed, thoroughly mix together by hand to blend fish together.
5. Using **steel blade,** process remaining carrot and ½ onion together until finely chopped. Remove half of this mixture from the bowl.
6. Add half of fish mixture to the bowl. To this add 1 egg, 3 tablespoons ice water, 2 tablespoons matzoh meal, 1 teaspoon salt, and ¼ teaspoon pepper. Process, using quick on/off motions, until thoroughly blended. Remove mixture from bowl and repeat procedure, using remaining ingredients.
7. Remove head, bones, and skin of fish from stock.
8. With wet hands, shape fish into shapes the size of a small baking potato and place in fish stock. Simmer slowly 2 hours.
9. Remove fish balls with a slotted spoon and place on a lettuce-lined platter. Cool and chill. Cool fish stock and save for later use for storing leftover fish.
10. Garnish with pieces of cooked carrots left over from stock and serve with freshly made horseradish.

*About 20 balls*

## Horseradish

½ cup horseradish root, cut in 1-inch cubes
Beet juice

Using **steel blade,** process until finely chopped. Add a few drops of beet juice to get desired color. Step back from bowl before removing lid!

# Eggplant Caviar

1 large eggplant (2 pounds)
1 clove garlic
1 large onion, peeled and quartered
1 small green pepper, trimmed and cut in 1-inch pieces
6 tablespoons olive oil
2 tablespoons tomato paste
2 teaspoons lemon juice
1 teaspoon salt
¼ teaspoon pepper

1. Bake eggplant in a 400°F oven for about 1 hour, or until skin is wrinkled and eggplant is soft. Cool.
2. Using **steel blade,** mince garlic. Add onion and green pepper and process until finely chopped.
3. In a skillet, sauté garlic, onion, and green pepper in 4 tablespoons olive oil until tender, but not browned.
4. When eggplant has cooled sufficiently to handle, remove the skin. Using **steel blade,** process until finely chopped.
5. Add chopped eggplant to skillet with onion mixture. Add 2 tablespoons oil and tomato paste and cook slowly, stirring occasionally, about 20 minutes.
6. Mix in lemon juice, salt, and pepper. Serve well chilled with **black bread.**

*Note:* The flavor of this dish improves on standing overnight. It keeps up to a week in the refrigerator.

From the Jewish dinner menu on page 8:
Gefilte Fish, 17

# Caraway Cheese Twists

2 ounces sharp Cheddar cheese
(1 cup shredded)
1 cup flour
¼ teaspoon salt
1 tablespoon shortening
8 tablespoons butter (1 stick), frozen
and cut in 6 pieces
1 tablespoon caraway seed
3 tablespoons ice water

1. Using **shredding disc,** shred cheese and set aside.
2. Using **steel blade,** add flour, salt, shortening, and butter to bowl and process until butter is cut into flour.
3. Add caraway seed and shredded cheese to bowl. With machine on, add water through feed tube and process until dough forms into a ball.
4. Roll dough ¼ inch thick and cut into strips 4×¾ inches. Twist strips and place on baking sheet.
5. Bake at 425°F about 15 minutes.

*About 3 dozen twists*

# Salmon Snowball

**Snowball:**
1 can (8 ounces) red salmon
8 tablespoon (1 stick) unsalted
butter, cut in 6 pieces
1 package (3 ounces) cream cheese,
cut in half
1 tablespoon lemon juice
2 pimentos (from jar)
1 teaspoon grated horseradish
1 teaspoon Worcestershire sauce
½ teaspoon salt
⅛ teaspoon pepper
Dash garlic powder

1. For snowball, drain salmon, reserving liquid, and remove any skin or bones.
2. Using **steel blade,** add all ingredients for snowball to the bowl and process until thoroughly blended and smooth.
3. Wet hands and shape into a ball. Refrigerate until firm.
4. For frosting, add cream cheese, salmon liquid, and lemon juice to bowl and process with **steel blade** until light and fluffy.
5. One hour before serving, frost the chilled salmon ball and return to refrigerator.
6. When ready to serve, garnish with parsley sprigs and accompany with **toast rounds** or **crackers.**

*1 large appetizer ball*

**Frosting:**
1 package (3 ounces) cream cheese,
cut in half
1 tablespoon reserved salmon liquid
1 teaspoon lemon juice
Parsley sprigs for garnish

# Spicy Steak Tartare

1 small green onion, cleaned,
trimmed, and cut in 1-inch
pieces
2 tablespoons fresh parsley, cleaned
and trimmed (1 tablespoon
chopped)
1 radish, cleaned and trimmed
½ pound beef (sirloin, tenderloin, or
fillet), cut in 1-inch cubes
1 egg yolk
1 tablespoon lemon juice
1 tablespoon capers
Drop of Dijon mustard
Salt
Freshly ground black pepper to
taste
3 drops Tabasco

Using **steel blade,** process green onion, parsley, and radish together until finely chopped. Add meat and remaining ingredients and process, using quick on/off motions, to desired consistency. Serve with triangles of **black bread.**

# Beef or Crab Meat Turnovers

**Pastry Dough:**
- 2 cups flour
- 8 tablespoons butter (1 stick), frozen and cut in 6 pieces
- 3 tablespoons shortening
- ½ teaspoon salt
- 6 tablespoons ice water
- Cream

**Beef Filling or Crab Meat Filling**

1. Using **steel blade,** add flour, butter, shortening, and salt to the bowl. Process until butter is cut into flour. With machine on, add water through the feed tube and process until dough forms into a ball.
2. Roll out dough to ⅛-inch thickness. Using a 3-inch round cookie cutter, cut out circles of dough. Place 1 heaping tablespoon of filling onto center of circle. Brush edges with cold water and add top crust. Press edges together with a fork. Brush tops with cream.
3. Bake at 425°F 15 to 20 minutes, or until puffy and lightly browned.

*About 3 dozen turnovers*

## Beef Filling

- 1 slice dry bread (¼ cup crumbs)
- ¼ cup fresh parsley, cleaned and trimmed (2 tablespoons chopped)
- 1 medium onion, peeled and quartered
- 2 tablespoons butter
- ½ pound beef, cut in 1-inch cubes
- ⅛ teaspoon marjoram
- ⅛ teaspoon basil
- ¼ teaspoon salt
- ⅛ teaspoon pepper
- 1 tablespoon flour
- ¼ cup cream

1. Using **steel blade,** separately process bread to fine crumbs, parsley until chopped, and onion until finely chopped. Set aside.
2. In a skillet, sauté onion in butter until transparent.
3. Still using **steel blade,** process meat until finely chopped and add it to the onion. Cook until meat is no longer pink.
4. Stir in seasonings and flour and cook for a minute or so. Add bread crumbs, chopped parsley, and cream. Cook until heated.

*Enough filling for 1½ dozen 3-inch turnovers*

## Crab Meat Filling

- 1 cube (2 inches) Swiss cheese
- 1 can (7 ounces) crab meat
- ¼ cup fresh parsley, cleaned and trimmed (2 tablespoons chopped)
- 2 green onions, cleaned and trimmed
- 1 apple, pared, cored, and quartered
- 2 tablespoons butter
- 1 tablespoon flour
- 2 tablespoons sherry
- 2 tablespoons cream
- ¼ teaspoon salt
- Dash pepper

1. Using **shredding disc,** shred cheese and set aside.
2. Drain crab meat, reserving liquid. Go over crab meat carefully and remove any tendons.
3. Using **steel blade,** separately process parsley until chopped, green onion until finely chopped, and apple until finely chopped.
4. In a saucepan, sauté green onion in butter until soft. Add chopped apple and cook until tender.
5. Sprinkle with flour and stir until bubbly; cook 1 to 2 minutes. Combine clam juice, sherry, and enough water to make ½ cup liquid. Add to flour mixture and stir until smooth.
6. Add crab meat, shredded cheese, parsley, cream, salt, and pepper. Heat thoroughly.

*Enough filling for 1½ dozen turnovers*

*Note:* Both of the above fillings make excellent canapé spreads. Cut homemade white bread into rounds and toast on one side. Spread filling on untoasted side. Top with a pinch of shredded cheese and a drop of melted butter. Set under a broiler for a few minutes until tops are lightly browned.

# Pepperoni and Cheese Canapés

1 piece (3 inches) pepperoni, cut in small pieces
4 ounces Cheddar cheese, cut in 1-inch cubes
1 package (3 ounces) cream cheese, cut in half
Toast rounds

1. Using **steel blade,** process pepperoni until coarsely chopped. Add Cheddar cheese and cream cheese and process together until thoroughly blended and smooth.
2. Spread on toast rounds and place under broiler for a few minutes until tops start to brown.

*Note:* This also makes an excellent spread to serve with crackers. For a thinner consistency, add about **1 tablespoon cream.**

# Cocktail Puffs

**Pastry for Puffs:**
1 cup water
8 tablespoons butter (1 stick), cut in 6 pieces
½ teaspoon salt
1 teaspoon sugar
Pinch nutmeg
1 cup flour
4 eggs

Beer-Cheddar Filling or Spread or Herb-Cheese Filling or Spread

1. In a saucepan, combine water, butter, salt, sugar, and nutmeg and bring to a boil.
2. Remove from heat and add flour all at once, stirring briskly with a wooden spoon until all ingredients are thoroughly combined and mixture pulls away from the sides of the pan and forms into a ball.
3. Remove pan from heat and let mixture stand 5 minutes.
4. Using **steel blade,** place ball of dough in bowl and add 4 eggs. Process until thoroughly blended, smooth, and shiny.
5. Using either a pastry bag or 2 teaspoons, drop 1-inch balls of dough on a buttered baking sheet.
6. Bake at 425°F about 20 minutes, or until golden brown.
7. To fill puffs, either cut off tops or slit the sides, and squeeze the spread or filling through a pastry bag into the puffs.

*About 3 dozen cocktail puffs*

*Note:* Puff shells freeze very well. Before ready to use, place them on baking sheet and heat in a 425°F oven 3 to 4 minutes, or until thawed and crispy.

## Beer-Cheddar Filling or Spread

8 ounces sharp Cheddar cheese, cut in 1-inch cubes
1 tablespoon Worcestershire sauce
½ teaspoon Dijon mustard
½ cup beer

1. Using **steel blade,** process cheese until finely chopped.
2. Add Worcestershire sauce, mustard, and beer and process until creamy and smooth.
3. Use as a filling for cocktail puffs or as a spread for crackers.

## Herb-Cheese Filling or Spread

1 small clove garlic
1 package (8 ounces) cream cheese, cut in quarters
8 tablespoons butter (1 stick), softened and cut in 6 pieces
1 tablespoon fresh parsley
¼ teaspoon oregano
¼ teaspoon thyme
¼ teaspoon basil

1. Using **steel blade,** mince garlic. Add remaining ingredients to the bowl and process until creamy and smooth.
2. Use as a filling for cocktail puffs or as a spread for crackers.

# Clam Canapés

¼ cup fresh parsley, cleaned and
  trimmed (2 tablespoons chopped)
4 ounces Cheddar cheese, cut in
  1-inch cubes
1 package (3 ounces) cream cheese,
  cut in half
1 can (8 ounces) minced clams
  Toast rounds

1. Using **steel blade,** process parsley until chopped; set aside.
2. Still using **steel blade,** add Cheddar cheese to bowl and process until finely chopped. Add cream cheese and process until smooth and creamy.
3. Drain clams, reserving juice. Add clams, parsley, and 1 tablespoon or more of clam juice and process, using quick on/off motions, until clams are incorporated into cheese. There should be chunks of cheese throughout the mixture.
4. Spread on toast rounds and broil for a few minutes until cheese starts to brown.

*Note:* Shrimp or crab meat can be added for a tasty variation.

# Bacon-Cheese Puffs

12 slices bacon
 3 ounces Swiss cheese (1½ cups
   shredded)
 2 cups Pastry for Puffs (see recipe
   for Cocktail Puffs, page 20)

1. Cook bacon until crisp. Drain well on paper towels. Using **steel blade,** process bacon until finely chopped; set aside.
2. Using **shredding disc,** shred cheese and set aside.
3. Make pastry dough. After eggs have been added, add cheese and bacon to warm mixture and process until blended.
4. Bake as for Cocktail Puffs.

*Note:* These puffs do not rise as much as the others do, nor do they need a filling. They are tasty just the way they are.

# Sweet and Sour Meatball Appetizers

*Meatballs:*
    4 slices dry bread, cut in quarters
      (1 cup crumbs)
    ½ small onion, peeled and cut in
      half
  1½ pounds beef, cut in 1-inch cubes
    2 eggs
    2 teaspoons Worcestershire sauce
    1 teaspoon salt
    ½ teaspoon pepper
    2 tablespoons butter

*Sauce:*
    1 medium onion, peeled and
      quartered
    1 medium carrot, pared and cut in
      1-inch pieces
    1 medium apple, pared, cored, and
      quartered
    1 can (6 ounces) tomato paste
    ¼ cup firmly packed brown sugar
    ½ cup apricot preserves
    1 teaspoon salt
    1 tablespoon lemon juice
    2 cups water

1. For meatballs, using **steel blade,** separately process bread to fine crumbs and onion until finely chopped. Also using **steel blade,** process ½ pound meat at a time, using quick on/off motions, until finely chopped. Remove each portion from the bowl and set aside.
2. Using **plastic blade,** put half of chopped meat mixture into the bowl. To this add ½ cup bread crumbs, half of chopped onion, 1 egg, 1 teaspoon Worcestershire sauce, ½ teaspoon salt, and ¼ teaspoon pepper. Process, with quick on/off motions, until thoroughly blended. Remove from bowl and repeat procedure, using remainder of ingredients.
3. Shape meat mixture into 1-inch balls.
4. In a large skillet, melt butter and brown meatballs on all sides over medium-high heat.
5. For sauce, using **steel blade,** add onion, carrot, and apple to bowl and process all together until finely chopped. Add tomato paste, brown sugar, apricot preserves, salt, and lemon juice; process until smooth. With machine on, add water through feed tube and process until blended.
6. Pour sauce over browned meatballs. Cover and simmer slowly about 45 minutes.
7. Serve in a chafing dish with wooden picks.

*About 60 cocktail meatballs*

# Egg Rolls

**Skins:**
>    1½  **cups flour**
>    ½  **teaspoon salt**
>    2  **eggs, fork beaten**
>    1½  **cups water**

**Filling:**
>    ¼  **pound cooked roast pork, cut in 1-inch cubes**
>    6  **medium shrimp, shelled and cooked**
>    3  **green onions, trimmed and cut in 1-inch pieces**
>    ½  **cup water chestnuts, drained**
>    3  **stalks celery, cut in 3-inch pieces**
>    4 to 6  **leaves Chinese cabbage**
>    ½  **cup bean sprouts, drained**
>    2  **tablespoons peanut oil**
>    1  **tablespoon soy sauce**
>    1  **tablespoon sherry**
>    ½  **teaspoon salt**
>    ½  **teaspoon sugar**

1. For skins, with **steel blade** in bowl, add flour and salt.
2. Combine lightly beaten eggs and water. With machine on, add liquid ingredients through the feed tube and process a few seconds until batter is smooth.
3. Lightly grease a 7- or 8-inch skillet with peanut oil and heat over medium heat until it smokes. Quickly pour exactly 2 tablespoons batter into the center of the pan and rotate to evenly spread the batter into a 5-inch circle. Cook about 2 minutes, until the edges of the pancake begin to curl. Remove to a plate and cover with a damp cloth. Repeat procedure until all batter is used, stacking skins on plate. If not using a well-seasoned pan, it will be necessary to lightly grease the skillet before making each skin.
4. Let skins cool completely before filling and rolling.

5. For filling, using **steel blade,** separately process pork and shrimp, using quick on/off motions, until coarsely chopped. Set aside.
6. Still using **steel blade,** process green onions until finely chopped. Set aside.
7. Using **shredding disc,** separately shred water chestnuts and celery, removing each from bowl; pack celery vertically in the feed tube, filling it as full as possible.
8. To slice Chinese cabbage, lightly roll together 2 to 3 leaves of cabbage and place vertically in feed tube. Slice with **slicing disc,** using light pressure.
9. Combine shredded celery, sliced Chinese cabbage, and bean sprouts in a bowl. These ingredients must be blanched before proceeding. To do so, cover with boiling water, stir a few times only, and remove to a colander. Immediately rinse with cold water and drain thoroughly. Roll ingredients in a towel to remove any excess moisture. Set aside.
10. Heat peanut oil in a wok. Add chopped pork and shrimp and stir-fry to heat through. Add remaining ingredients and stir-fry very briefly to heat through. Remove to a colander and let cool completely.
11. For rolls, skins and fillings must be completely cooled for successful egg rolls.
12. Place 2 to 3 tablespoons of filling slightly below the center of the skin. Fold the bottom side up to cover filling. Fold in sides and roll the skin. Brush the top edge with unbeaten egg white and seal like an envelope.
13. To cook, heat ¼-inch peanut oil in a large skillet and fry on both sides until lightly browned. Drain on paper towels.

*About 15 egg rolls*

*Note:* Egg rolls can be made in advance. To reheat, place in 325°F oven for 10 to 15 minutes.

# SOUPS

# Shrimp Dumplings in Chicken Broth

1 slice ginger
1 green onion, cut in
    1-inch pieces
½ pound fresh shrimp, shelled and
    deveined
1 egg white
½ teaspoon cornstarch
1 tablespoon sherry
2 teaspoons soy sauce
¼ teaspoon salt
8 cups chicken stock

1. Using **steel blade,** with machine on, drop ginger slice down through the feed tube and process until minced.
2. Add green onion pieces and process until finely chopped.
3. Add shrimp and process until of a pastelike consistency. Add egg white, cornstarch, sherry, soy sauce, and salt and process until thoroughly blended.
4. In a large shallow saucepan, heat chicken stock to boiling and simmer over low heat. Using two teaspoons, drop 1-inch balls of batter into simmering chicken stock. Cover and cook over medium heat until done (about 8 to 10 minutes).
5. Just before serving, garnish soup with **sliced green onion.**

*About 30 (1-inch) balls or*
*8 servings*

# Block Island Quahog Chowder

1 cube (2 inches) salt pork, partially
    frozen
1 large onion, peeled and quartered
2 to 3 medium potatoes, pared and
    diced
¼ teaspoon pepper
2 dozen large quahogs (hard-shelled
    clams)

1. Using **slicing disc,** slice salt pork. In a large saucepan, cook salt pork until browned.
2. Using **steel blade,** process onion until finely chopped. Add onion to crisp salt pork and cook until onion is transparent. Remove salt pork and discard.
3. Cook diced potatoes in 1 quart water, with pepper added, until almost tender. Do not drain.
4. Meanwhile, rinse quahogs well and open with a clam knife. (If you are not adept at opening clams in this manner, see Note for an alternate method.) Be sure that all the juice is retained. Strain quahogs, and add reserved juice to saucepan with cooked onions. Using **steel blade,** process clams in two batches until finely chopped. Add to saucepan.
5. Add cooked potatoes and water they were cooked in. Add 2 cups water, more or less, if the flavor is too strong. Simmer 15 to 20 minutes but do not boil. Serve with **chowder crackers.**

*8 to 10 servings*

*Note:* An alternate method for opening clams: Rinse clams thoroughly under cold water. Place clams in a saucepan and add 2 cups water. Cook, covered, over medium heat only until shells start to open. Remove clams, reserving clam broth for chowder. Remove clams from shells and proceed as above.

# Escarole Soup with Tiny Meatballs

**Soup:**
4 pounds beef soup bones
1 can (6 ounces) tomato paste
2½ teaspoons salt
2 quarts water
1 pound escarole, cleaned and
    drained

1. For soup, put all ingredients, except escarole, into a saucepot. Cover and simmer for 1 hour. Remove bones.

2. For meatballs, using **steel blade,** separately process bread to fine crumbs, Parmesan cheese to fine powder, and parsley until chopped; set aside. Next, mince garlic. Add meat in two batches and process until finely chopped and remove to bowl.
3. Using **plastic blade,** add chopped meat, egg, salt, pepper,

*Meatballs:*
- 1 slice dry bread, cut in quarters (¼ cup crumbs)
- 2 cubes (1 inch each) Parmesan cheese (¼ cup grated)
- ¼ cup fresh parsley, cleaned and trimmed (2 tablespoons chopped)
- 1 clove garlic
- ¾ pound beef, cut in 1-inch cubes
- 1 egg
- ½ teaspoon salt
- ¼ teaspoon pepper

bread crumbs, Parmesan cheese, and chopped parsley to bowl. Process, using quick on/off motions, until thoroughly blended.

4. Shape into ¾-inch balls and add to hot soup. Simmer 10 minutes.

5. Using **steel blade**, process escarole, using quick on/off motions, until coarsely chopped. Add escarole to soup and simmer 30 minutes longer.

*8 servings*

# Greens Soup

- 2 cubes (1 inch each) Parmesan cheese (¼ cup grated)
- 1 pound mixed greens (lettuce, spinach, watercress, as well as any others), cleaned and trimmed
- 6 tablespoons butter
- 3 tablespoons flour
- 1 quart chicken stock, heated
- 2 egg yolks
- 1 cup milk

1. Using **steel blade**, separately process Parmesan cheese to a fine powder, and greens (in small batches) until coarsely chopped.

2. Sauté greens in 2 tablespoons butter for a few minutes until wilted.

3. Meanwhile, in another saucepan, melt remaining 4 tablespoons butter, add flour, and cook for 5 minutes. Add heated stock, stirring with a whisk until smooth. Add greens, cover, and simmer for 20 minutes.

4. Strain soup. Purée vegetable mixture with **steel blade** until smooth and return to soup. Heat thoroughly and remove from heat.

5. With **plastic blade** in bowl, process egg yolks and milk together. With machine on, add 1 cup hot soup through feed tube and then add all of egg mixture to soup, stirring thoroughly. Add Parmesan cheese and simmer 5 minutes, being careful not to let soup boil after egg yolks have been added.

*6 servings*

# Cranberry-Beet Borscht

- 1½ cups whole cranberries
- 5 cups chicken stock
- 2 medium onions, peeled and quartered
- ½ small head cabbage
- 1 tablespoon sugar
- 1 can (8 ounces) whole beets and juice

1. Wash cranberries. In a large saucepan, combine cranberries and chicken stock and cook about 20 minutes, or until cranberries are soft. Sieve cranberries and return liquid to saucepan. Using **steel blade**, process sieved cranberries until puréed and return to saucepan.

2. Using **steel blade**, process onions until chopped. Add to saucepan.

3. Using **slicing disc**, slice cabbage and add to saucepan. Add sugar and simmer uncovered for about 20 minutes.

4. Just before serving, drain beets, adding juice to pan. Shred beets with **shredding disc** and add also. Simmer until thoroughly heated. Serve with a dollop of **dairy sour cream.**

*6 servings*

*Note:* This borscht can also be served chilled.

# Cream of Carrot Soup

6 **large carrots, pared and cut in**
    **1-inch pieces**
1 **onion, peeled and quartered**
1 **stalk celery, trimmed and cut in**
    **1-inch pieces**
4 **tablespoons butter**
2 **tablespoons flour**
6 **cups chicken stock**
¼ **cup uncooked rice**
1 **tablespoon sugar**
    **Pinch nutmeg**
1 **cup whipping cream**

1. Using **steel blade,** process carrots, onion, and celery together until finely chopped.
2. In a large saucepan, sauté chopped vegetables in butter for about 15 minutes. Stir in flour and cook for 2 minutes.
3. Gradually add chicken stock and rice, stirring constantly with a whisk until smooth. Cook slowly for 45 minutes, or until carrots and rice are tender.
4. Strain soup, returning liquid to saucepan. Using **steel blade,** process carrot mixture until puréed and return to saucepan. Add sugar and nutmeg. Bring to a boil, add ½ cup cream, and heat thoroughly.
5. Using a mixer, whip remaining cream. Serve each portion of soup with a dollop of whipped cream.

*8 servings*

# Leek and Potato Soup

1 **pound potatoes, pared and cut to**
    **fit feed tube**
1 **pound leeks, cleaned and cut in**
    **3½-inch pieces**
2 **quarts chicken stock**
½ **cup whipping cream**
    **Chopped parsley for garnish**

1. Using **slicing disc,** slice potatoes and leeks.
2. Put vegetables and chicken stock into a saucepan, partially cover, and cook for 30 minutes, or until vegetables are tender. Strain vegetables, reserving liquid.
3. Using **steel blade,** process vegetables to a smooth purée.
4. Add vegetable purée to reserved liquid and reheat to a simmer. Off heat and just before serving, stir in cream.
5. Garnish with parsley.

*About 12 servings*

# Cream of Green Onion Soup

1 **clove garlic**
2 **bunches green onions, trimmed and**
    **cut in 1-inch pieces**
4 **tablespoons butter**
3 **tablespoons flour**
5 **cups hot chicken stock**
1 **cup whipping cream**
    **Chopped parsley for garnish**

1. Using **steel blade,** mince garlic. Add green onions and process until finely chopped.
2. Sauté garlic and green onions in butter until tender but not brown. Stir in flour and cook about 2 minutes.
3. Gradually add chicken stock, stirring constantly with a whisk until smooth. Simmer for 30 minutes.
4. Strain soup. If desired, using **steel blade,** process green onion until puréed and add to soup.
5. Just before serving, add ½ cup cream and simmer until thoroughly heated.
6. Using a mixer, whip remaining cream. Serve each portion with a dollop of whipped cream. Sprinkle with chopped parsley.

*6 servings*

# Onion Cream Soup

5 large onions, peeled and quartered
1 stalk celery, trimmed and cut in
    1-inch pieces
4 tablespoons butter
1 large potato, pared and cut to fit
    feed tube
5 cups beef stock
1 cup dry white wine
1 tablespoon vinegar
2 teaspoons sugar
1 cup whipping cream

1. Using **steel blade,** process onions and celery in two batches until coarsely chopped.
2. Heat butter in a large saucepan. Add chopped onion and celery and cook until soft.
3. Using **slicing disc,** slice potato.
4. When onions are transparent, add beef stock and potato to pan. Cover, bring to a boil, and simmer 30 minutes.
5. Strain soup, returning liquid to saucepan. Using **steel blade,** process onion mixture until puréed. Return onion purée to saucepan. Add wine, vinegar, and sugar. Bring to boiling, reduce heat, and simmer 5 minutes.
6. Just before serving, add cream and adjust seasonings. Heat thoroughly, being careful not to boil.

*6 to 8 servings*

# Pumpkin Soup

1½ pounds fresh pumpkin, pared and
    cut to fit feed tube (2 cups
    puréed)
½ small onion, peeled and cut in
    half
2 tablespoons butter
2 cups chicken stock
2 cups milk
    Pinch cloves, ginger, and allspice
½ cup whipping cream
¼ cup sherry (optional)
    Whipped cream for garnish

1. Using **slicing disc,** slice pumpkin. Cook in salted water until tender and drain thoroughly. Set aside.
2. Using **steel blade,** process onion until coarsely chopped. Melt butter in a large saucepan and cook chopped onion until transparent.
3. Add chicken stock, cooked pumpkin, milk, and spices. Mix ingredients well and bring mixture to boiling. Reduce heat and simmer 20 minutes.
4. Using **steel blade,** add half of mixture to bowl and process until puréed. Process remaining half in same manner and return purée to saucepan.
5. Add cream and, if desired, sherry. Heat thoroughly, being careful not to boil. Serve garnished with whipped cream.

*6 servings*

*Note:* This soup can also be served chilled. Also, squash can be substituted for pumpkin.

# Curried Tomato Soup

2 stalks celery, cut in 1-inch pieces
½ green pepper, trimmed and cut in
    1-inch pieces
1 small onion, peeled and quartered
1 carrot, pared and cut in 1-inch
    pieces
4 tablespoons butter
2 tablespoons flour
4½ cups chicken stock
1 can (28 ounces) whole tomatoes
1 teaspoon curry powder
1 teaspoon salt
¼ teaspoon pepper

1. Using **steel blade,** process celery, green pepper, onion, and carrot all together until finely chopped.
2. In a large saucepan, sauté vegetables in butter until tender. Stir in flour and cook about 2 minutes. Gradually add chicken stock, stirring until smooth.
3. Drain tomatoes, adding liquid to pan. Using **steel blade,** process tomatoes until finely chopped and add to pan along with seasonings.
4. Bring to boiling, then lower heat and simmer 20 to 30 minutes.
5. Strain soup. Return soup to saucepan and add vegetables to bowl with **steel blade.** Process until puréed.
6. With machine running, add 2 cups of soup through feed tube and process until smooth. Return mixture to pot and cook until thoroughly heated.

*8 servings*

# Swiss Vegetable Soup

6 slices bacon
1 medium onion, peeled
1 leek, cleaned and trimmed
½ small head cabbage
2 small potatoes, pared
4 cups chicken stock
2 ounces Swiss cheese (1 cup shredded)
1 cup half-and-half
½ teaspoon dill weed

1. In a large saucepan, sauté bacon for 5 minutes.
2. Meanwhile, using **slicing disc,** slice onion, leek, and cabbage. Add to bacon and sauté for 5 minutes more.
3. Still using **slicing disc,** slice potatoes. Add potatoes and chicken stock to saucepan, bring to boiling, lower heat, and simmer uncovered for 40 minutes.
4. Strain vegetables, returning liquid to saucepan. Using **steel blade,** process vegetables until puréed. Return to saucepan.
5. Using **shredding disc,** shred cheese and add to soup. Stir over medium heat until melted. Do not boil. Just before serving, add half-and-half and dill.

*6 servings*

# Cheddar Cheese Soup

1 carrot, pared and cut in 1-inch pieces
1 stalk celery, cut in 1-inch pieces
½ small green pepper, trimmed and cut in 1-inch pieces
½ small onion, peeled and cut in half
8 tablespoons butter (1 stick)
4 ounces sharp Cheddar cheese (2 cups shredded)
⅓ cup flour
½ teaspoon dry mustard
2½ cups milk, heated
1 cup chicken stock
6 ounces beer (¾ cup)
½ teaspoon salt

1. Using **steel blade,** process carrot, celery, green pepper, and onion together until finely chopped. Sauté in 4 tablespoons butter until tender.
2. Using **shredding disc,** shred cheese and set aside.
3. In a large saucepan, melt remaining butter, add flour and dry mustard, and cook for 1 or 2 minutes. Add milk, stock, beer, and salt, stirring until thickened and smooth. Add sautéed vegetables and shredded cheese and stir until cheese is melted. Simmer for 15 to 20 minutes.
4. Strain soup and return strained liquid to pot. Process strained vegetables with **steel blade** until puréed, and return to saucepan. Simmer until thoroughly heated.

*6 servings*

# Cherry Soup

2 pounds frozen Bing cherries, thawed
7 cups water
½ cup sugar
1 stick cinnamon
1 long strip of lemon peel
3 tablespoons lemon juice
2 tablespoons cornstarch
¼ cup white wine

1. Drain cherries, reserving liquid. Set aside 1 cup whole cherries.
2. Add remaining cherries and cherry juice to water in large pot and cook 20 minutes, or until soft. Strain cherries from liquid. Add to bowl with **steel blade** and process until puréed. Put mixture through a fine sieve.
3. Return smooth purée to saucepan, add sugar, cinnamon, lemon peel, and lemon juice.
4. Dissolve cornstarch in white wine. Add it to soup, stirring so that soup remains smooth as it thickens. Add whole cherries and simmer 15 minutes. Serve soup either hot or chilled with a dollop of **dairy sour cream.**

*8 servings*

# Peanut Butter Soup

1 **medium onion, peeled and quartered**
2 **stalks celery, trimmed and cut in 1-inch pieces**
4 **tablespoons butter**
3 **tablespoons flour**
4 **cups milk**
1½ **cups chicken stock**
12 **ounces peanuts**
6 **slices bacon**

1. Using **steel blade,** process onion and celery together until finely chopped. Heat butter in a large saucepan and sauté until tender.
2. Stir in flour and cook for a few minutes. Add milk and chicken stock gradually, stirring with a whisk until smooth. Bring to boiling; cook and stir 1 to 2 minutes.
3. Using **steel blade,** add peanuts to bowl and process for a few minutes until peanut butter is smooth and creamy.
4. With machine on and peanut butter still in the bowl, add 2 cups soup through the feed tube and process until thoroughly blended, stopping to scrape the sides of bowl if necessary. Return mixture to saucepan and stir until well blended. Heat thoroughly.
5. Cook bacon until crisp. Using **steel blade,** process bacon, using quick on/off motions, until finely chopped.
6. Ladle hot soup into bowls and top with chopped crisp bacon.

*6 servings*

# German Shrimp Bisque

½ **small onion, peeled and cut in half**
1 **stalk celery, trimmed and cut in 1-inch pieces**
1 **pound shrimp (in shells)**
2 **quarts water**
2 **teaspoons salt**
1 **teaspoon caraway seed**
½ **teaspoon fennel**
3 **tablespoons butter**
¾ **cup flour**
4 **egg yolks**
1 **cup cream**
¼ **cup sherry**

1. Using **steel blade,** process onion and celery together until finely chopped and set aside.
2. In a large pot, combine shrimp, water, salt, caraway seed, fennel, and chopped onion and celery. Cook until shrimp is pink.
3. Drain shrimp, reserving stock. Shell and devein shrimp.
4. Using **steel blade,** process shrimp until finely chopped and sauté in butter for about 2 minutes. Stir in flour and cook for 1 minute. Slowly stir in reserved stock.
5. Bring to boiling, stirring constantly until smooth. Lower heat and simmer 15 minutes.
6. Strain soup, return liquid to pot, and add strained mixture to bowl with **steel blade.** Process for a few minutes until puréed to a smooth consistency. With machine running, add 2 cups soup through feed tube and process until smooth. If desired, strain again for a smoother consistency. Return mixture to pot.
7. Using **steel blade,** add egg yolks to bowl and beat lightly. With machine running, add 1 cup broth (soup) through feed tube. Then return mixture to pot. Stir in cream and sherry and simmer until thoroughly heated.

*8 servings*

# Chilled Avocado Soup

2 large or 4 small avocados, peeled
   and cubed
2 cups chicken stock
1½ cups whipping cream
½ cup dry white wine
1 tablespoon lemon juice
½ teaspoon salt
   Whipped cream or dairy sour
    cream for garnish

1. Using **steel blade,** process avocado until puréed, stopping occasionally to scrape down sides (you should have 2 cups of purée).
2. With machine on, add chicken stock through feed tube and process until smooth.
3. Remove mixture to a bowl and add remaining ingredients, mixing well. Chill before serving.
4. Serve with a dollop of whipped cream or sour cream.

*6 servings*

# Gazpacho

2 large carrots, pared and cut in
   1-inch pieces
3 stalks celery, cut in 1-inch pieces
1 medium green pepper, trimmed
   and cut in 1-inch pieces
1 medium cucumber, pared and
   seeded and cut in 1-inch pieces
3 large tomatoes, cut in quarters
1 clove garlic
1 can (32 ounces) tomato juice
¼ cup salad oil
2 tablespoons lemon juice
1 teaspoon Worcestershire sauce
1 tablespoon sugar
1 teaspoon salt
   Toasted croutons

1. Using **steel blade,** separately process carrots, celery, green pepper, cucumber, and tomatoes until chopped to desired consistency and remove to a large bowl or container with a cover.
2. Add remaining ingredients to chopped vegetables. Mix and refrigerate at least 24 hours. Remove garlic. Serve with toasted croutons.

*6 to 8 servings*

# MAIN DISHES

# Beef Rouladen with Spätzle

2½ pounds beef round steak
8 slices bacon
2 slices fresh pumpernickel (1 cup crumbs)
1 cup fresh parsley, cleaned and trimmed (½ cup chopped)
4 medium onions, peeled and quartered
2 tablespoons capers
2 whole dill pickles
Dijon mustard
3 tablespoons butter
Flour
2 carrots, pared and cut in 1-inch pieces
2 stalks celery, trimmed and cut in 1-inch pieces
2 cups beef stock
½ cup red wine
¼ cup tomato paste or purée (or ketchup)

Spätzle

1. Pound meat into paper-thin slices. Cut into pieces, approximately 3×5 inches. There should be about 12 to 16 such pieces.
2. Cook bacon until crisp, drain well, and set aside, reserving 2 tablespoons bacon drippings.
3. Using **steel blade,** separately process bread to fine crumbs, parsley until chopped, and 2 onions until chopped. Remove each from bowl and set aside.
4. In a large skillet, sauté chopped onion in bacon drippings until golden. Add bread crumbs and chopped parsley and cook for 5 minutes.
5. Using **steel blade,** process cooked bacon until finely chopped. Add bread-crumb mixture and capers and process until blended.
6. Cut pickles in lengthwise quarters and then in half again to make eighths.
7. Spread each meat slice with a little mustard. Spread 1 rounded tablespoon of bread-crumb mixture on each slice, place a piece of pickle in the middle, and roll tightly. Secure with wooden picks or tie with string.
8. Dredge each beef roll in flour and brown in butter, turning to cook on both sides. Remove and set aside.
9. Still using **steel blade,** process carrots, celery, and remaining 2 onions together until finely chopped. Add to pan and cook for about 5 minutes until golden. Place beef rolls on top; add beef stock, wine, and tomato paste and simmer covered 1½ hours, or until tender.
10. When done, remove beef rolls. Strain sauce, reserving liquid. Put cooked vegetable mixture in bowl with **steel blade** and process until puréed. Add strained liquid through feed tube with machine on and process until blended.
11. Return to pot, add beef rolls, and reheat before serving. Serve with Spätzle.

*6 to 8 servings*

## Spätzle

2 eggs
2½ cups flour
1 teaspoon salt
½ cup water

1. Using **steel blade,** add eggs to bowl and beat lightly. Add flour and salt and process together for a few seconds.
2. With machine on, add water through feed tube and process until mixture forms into a ball. Once this occurs, let ball of dough spin about 15 to 20 seconds.
3. Roll dough out to ⅛-inch thickness. With a sharp knife, trim off thin slivers of dough about 3 inches in length. Transfer to a plate and push into a large pot of boiling salted water. Do not overcrowd. Cook in several batches for 10 to 15 minutes, or until tender. Remove with a slotted spoon to a colander and drain. Transfer to a bowl and toss with melted butter. Keep warm while cooking remainder of dough.

*About 4 cups*

*Note:* Spätzle can be added to a soup or served as a side dish with meat. In the latter case, gently toss with melted butter. Toasted bread crumbs, and/or grated Parmesan cheese can also be added for a tasty variation.

From the Mexican dinner menu on page 8:
Green Chili Cornbread, 81, Guacamole, 16, and
Mexican Picadillo with Rice, 34

# Stuffed Flank Steak

6 slices dry bread, cut in quarters (1½ cups crumbs)
4 cubes (1 inch each) Parmesan cheese (½ cup grated)
½ cup fresh parsley, cleaned and trimmed (¼ cup chopped)
1 clove garlic
2½ medium onions, peeled and quartered
2 tablespoons butter
¼ pound mushrooms, cleaned and trimmed
¼ teaspoon tarragon
½ teaspoon salt
¼ teaspoon pepper
1 egg
1 beef flank steak (about 2 pounds)
1 carrot, pared and cut in 1-inch pieces
1 stalk celery, cut in 1-inch pieces
½ cup red wine
1 cup beef stock

1. Using **steel blade,** separately process bread to coarse crumbs, Parmesan cheese to a fine powder, and parsley until chopped; remove from bowl.
2. Still using **steel blade,** mince garlic. Add 2 onions and process until chopped.
3. In a skillet, heat butter and sauté onion and garlic until lightly browned.
4. Using **steel blade,** process mushrooms until chopped and add to skillet along with tarragon, salt, pepper, and parsley; cook a few minutes more.
5. Using **plastic blade,** lightly beat egg. Add bread crumbs and mushroom mixture to bowl and process, with quick on/off motions, until blended.
6. Spread the mixture on the steak. Roll lengthwise in a jelly-roll fashion and tie with string at 1-inch intervals.
7. In a heavy skillet or Dutch oven, brown the meat on all sides and remove from pan.
8. Using **steel blade,** process carrot, celery, and remaining ½ onion together until finely chopped. Add to skillet, along with wine and beef stock. Place stuffed flank steak on top and cover tightly.
9. Bake at 350°F about 2 hours, or until tender.
10. When meat is done, remove from pan, and keep warm. Using **steel blade,** process pan drippings until puréed. Add more water or milk to reach desired consistency.
11. Put steak on a platter and surround with cooked vegetables such as **sliced zucchini, julienne carrots,** and **frenched green beans.**
12. Cut steak into 1-inch slices and serve with gravy on the side.

*4 to 6 servings*

# Beef Brisket

1 beef brisket (4 to 5 pounds)
2 tablespoons chicken fat
2 cloves garlic
5 medium onions, peeled and quartered
¼ teaspoon dry mustard
½ teaspoon rosemary
¼ teaspoon thyme
¼ cup ketchup
1 bay leaf
1 teaspoon brown sugar
1 tablespoon paprika
1 tablespoon salt
2 cups water
½ pound mushrooms, cleaned and trimmed
½ cup sherry

1. In a roasting pan, brown meat on both sides in chicken fat.
2. Using **steel blade,** mince garlic and leave in bowl.
3. Using **slicing disc,** slice onions. Put onions and garlic on bottom of roasting pan. Place meat on top.
4. Combine remaining ingredients, except mushrooms and sherry. Pour over meat and cover.
5. Cook in a 350°F oven for 2 hours.
6. Using **slicing disc,** slice mushrooms. Add sherry and mushrooms and cook 1 hour longer, or until meat is tender. (More water can be added as liquid cooks down. Potatoes can also be added the last hour.)

*8 servings*

From the Greek dinner menu on page 8:
Greek Salad, 67, Greek Sesame Bread, 77, and Moussaka, 42

# Beef with Pea Pods and Water Chestnuts

½ pound beef (round steak or flank steak), cut to fit feed tube and partially frozen (cut blocks of meat so that they will be sliced against the grain)
4 green onions, trimmed
½ cup water chestnuts, drained
½ pound pea pods, stemmed and stringed
1 clove garlic
1 tablespoon cornstarch
1 teaspoon sugar
2 tablespoons oyster sauce
2 teaspoons soy sauce
3 tablespoons cold water
3 tablespoons peanut oil
1 tablespoon sherry
½ cup beef stock

1. Using **slicing disc**, slice meat (page 13). Set aside.
2. Still using **slicing disc**, pack feed tube as full as possible with green onions. They can be placed either horizontally (to yield slivers) or vertically (to yield slices). Slice and set aside for garnish.
3. Still using **slicing disc**, slice water chestnuts and set aside.
4. Parboil pea pods for 2 minutes. Rinse immediately with cold water and drain.
5. Using **steel blade**, mince garlic.
6. Blend cornstarch, sugar, oyster sauce, 1 teaspoon soy sauce, and cold water.
7. Heat 1½ tablespoons peanut oil in a wok. Add minced garlic and stir-fry to brown lightly. Add beef and stir-fry until no longer red (about 2 minutes). Remove from wok.
8. Heat 1½ tablespoons peanut oil in wok. Add pea pods and water chestnuts and stir-fry 2 minutes. Return beef. Add sherry and 1 teaspoon soy sauce and stir-fry for 1 minute more. Add stock and heat quickly.
9. Stir in cornstarch mixture to thicken. Remove to a serving dish, sprinkle with sliced or slivered green onions. Serve immediately with **rice** or **Chinese noodles.**

*4 servings*

# Mexican Picadillo

½ cup fresh parsley, cleaned and trimmed (¼ cup chopped)
1 clove garlic
1 pound beef, cut in 1-inch cubes
1 pound pork, cut in 1-inch cubes
2 onions, peeled and quartered
1 green pepper, trimmed and cut in 1-inch pieces
1 tablespoon oil
1 apple, pared, cored, and quartered
1 stalk celery, trimmed and cut in 1-inch pieces
1 or more jalapeño peppers
1 can (28 ounces) whole tomatoes
½ cup raisins
½ cup dry red wine
⅛ teaspoon cinnamon
⅛ teaspoon cloves
⅛ teaspoon ginger
1½ teaspoons salt
¼ teaspoon pepper

1. Using **steel blade**, process parsley until chopped and set aside. Add garlic and process until minced. Add meat in ½-pound batches and process until finely chopped and set aside.
2. Still using **steel blade**, separately process onions and green pepper until chopped. In a large skillet, cook onion and green pepper in oil until soft. Add chopped meat and cook until no longer pink.
3. Still using **steel blade**, separately process apple and celery until chopped and add to meat mixture.
4. Drain jalapeño peppers and remove seeds. Using **steel blade**, process until finely chopped and add to meat mixture.
5. Drain tomatoes. Add juice to meat mixture and process tomatoes with **steel blade** until chopped. Add to meat.
6. Add remaining ingredients and simmer uncovered for 30 minutes longer until flavors are well blended and filling is slightly thickened.
7. Serve over a bed of **rice.**

*8 servings*

# Pork Ragout

3 pounds pork, cut in 1-inch cubes
2 tablespoons butter
2 tablespoons oil
½ cup fresh parsley, cleaned and trimmed (¼ cup chopped)
2 cloves garlic
1 medium onion, peeled and quartered
1 large carrot, pared and cut in 1-inch pieces
1 stalk celery, trimmed and cut in 1-inch pieces
1 can (28 ounces) whole tomatoes, drained
½ bay leaf
½ teaspoon thyme
1 teaspoon curry powder
1 cup beef stock
Salt and pepper to taste

1. In a large skillet or Dutch oven, sauté pork in butter and oil. Remove from skillet and set aside.
2. Using **steel blade,** separately process parsley until chopped; garlic, onion, carrot, and celery until finely chopped. In same skillet in which pork was cooked, sauté chopped vegetable mixture about 10 minutes and remove from skillet.
3. Using **steel blade,** process drained tomatoes until finely chopped.
4. Return pork to skillet, add chopped vegetables and parsley, top with chopped tomatoes, and add bay leaf, thyme, curry powder, salt, pepper, and beef stock; gently mix. Cover skillet.
5. Bake at 375°F about 1 hour, or until pork is tender. Serve with **Saffron Rice** (page 41) or **noodles.**

*6 servings*

# Stuffed Pork Chops with Sour Cream

4 slices dry bread, cut in quarters (1 cup crumbs)
2 cubes (1 inch each) Parmesan cheese (¼ cup grated)
¼ cup fresh parsley (2 tablespoons chopped)
2 green onions, cut in 1-inch pieces
¼ pound mushrooms, cleaned and trimmed
4 tablespoons butter
1 egg
½ teaspoon tarragon
Salt and pepper
6 double loin pork chops with pockets
Flour for dredging
1 tablespoon oil
2 medium onions, peeled
1 cup chicken stock (about)
2 tablespoons sherry (optional)
1 cup dairy sour cream

1. Using **steel blade,** separately process bread to fine crumbs, Parmesan cheese to a fine powder, and parsley until chopped; remove from bowl.
2. Still using **steel blade,** process green onions until finely chopped.
3. In a skillet, melt 2 tablespoons butter and sauté green onions until tender.
4. Still using **steel blade,** process mushrooms, using quick on/off motions, until finely chopped. Add to green onions and cook until liquid is evaporated.
5. Using **plastic blade,** lightly beat egg. Add bread crumbs, Parmesan cheese, chopped parsley, mushroom mixture and tarragon and process until blended together. Season to taste with salt and pepper.
6. Stuff pork chops and tie together with string.
7. Dredge pork chops in flour. In a large skillet, brown chops on both sides in 2 tablespoons butter plus 1 tablespoon oil and remove from skillet.
8. Using **slicing disc,** slice onions and sauté for a couple of minutes in skillet. Return pork chops. Add enough stock to cover bottom of skillet about 1 inch. Cover skillet and cook 1 to 1½ hours, or until fork tender. Turn once.
9. When chops are tender, remove from skillet. Add sherry, if desired, and sour cream and stir together. Return pork chops and heat thoroughly, but do not boil. Serve with **buttered noodles** or **Spätzle** (page 32).

*6 servings*

# Barbecued Spareribs

3 pounds spareribs, cracked through
   the center
Salt and pepper
1 small green pepper, trimmed and
   cut in 1-inch pieces
1 small onion, peeled and quartered
1 stalk celery, peeled and cut in
   1-inch pieces
3 tablespoons butter
½ cup cider vinegar
½ cup ketchup
¼ cup brown sugar
1 tablespoon Worcestershire sauce
½ teaspoon dry mustard
½ teaspoon chili powder
2 lemon slices

1. Cut ribs into serving-size pieces, sprinkle with salt and pepper, and place, meaty side up, in a shallow roasting pan. Bake at 350°F 30 minutes, turning once.
2. Using **steel blade**, place green pepper, onion, and celery in bowl and process until coarsely chopped. In a saucepan, heat butter and sauté chopped vegetables until tender, stirring occasionally.
3. Return mixture to bowl with **steel blade**. Add remaining ingredients except lemon slices and process until puréed. Return to saucepan, add lemon slices, and simmer 10 minutes, stirring frequently. Remove from heat and set aside.
4. After ribs have baked for 30 minutes, remove them from oven and pour off excess fat. Spoon one half of the sauce over the ribs. Cover and continue baking, basting frequently, 1 to 1½ hours, or until meat is tender. Uncover the pan for the last 15 minutes.

*6 servings*

# Roast Duckling à l'Orange with Apricot-Rice Stuffing

**Duck:**
1 duckling (about 4 pounds)
1 teaspoon salt
1½ cups orange juice
3 tablespoons butter

**Apricot-Rice Stuffing:**
2 cups cooked rice (1 cup wild and
   1 cup white rice)
¼ cup fresh parsley, cleaned and
   trimmed (2 tablespoons
   chopped)
6 ounces dried apricots
1 small onion, peeled and quartered
1 stalk celery, trimmed and cut in
   1-inch pieces
¼ cup orange juice
3 tablespoons butter, melted
¼ teaspoon salt
⅛ teaspoon pepper
⅛ teaspoon nutmeg
⅛ teaspoon cloves

**Orange Sauce:**
1 tablespoon flour
2 oranges, sectioned
2 tablespoons orange liqueur
   (optional)
Salt and pepper to taste

1. Rinse duckling and pat dry with paper towel. Rub cavity with salt.
2. In a saucepan, heat orange juice and butter over low heat until butter is melted. Remove from heat and using a pastry brush, brush cavity with mixture.
3. For stuffing, using **steel blade**, separately process parsley, dried apricots, onion, and celery until finely chopped. Combine all ingredients for stuffing in a large bowl and toss until thoroughly mixed.
4. Lightly fill body and neck cavity with the stuffing. Do not pack. To close body cavity, sew or skewer and lace with a cord. Fasten neck skin to back and wings to body with skewers. Place duckling, breast up, on a rack in a roasting pan. Brush with juice mixture.
5. Roast, uncovered, at 325°F 2½ to 3 hours. Brush frequently with orange juice mixture. Pour off drippings as they accumulate. When duckling is done, drumstick should move easily.
6. Place duckling on a heated platter. Pour off fat from roasting pan, reserving 2 tablespoons, leaving brown residue in the bottom. Put reserved fat into roasting pan and blend in 1 tablespoon flour, stirring constantly over medium heat until mixture bubbles. Remove from heat and continue to stir while slowly adding remaining orange juice mixture and sectioned oranges. Return to heat and cook rapidly, stirring constantly, until gravy thickens. Cook 1 to 2 minutes longer, while stirring; scrape bottom and sides of pan to blend in brown residue. Add orange liqueur and/or more orange juice to reach desired consistency. Adjust seasonings. Remove from heat, pour into gravy boat, and serve hot with duckling.

*3 or 4 servings*

# Chilean Chicken

3 pounds chicken, cut in serving
    pieces
¾ cup flour
2 teaspoons salt
½ teaspoon pepper
2 tablespoons butter
2 tablespoons oil
1 clove garlic
1 large carrot, pared and cut in
    1-inch pieces
3 stalks celery, cleaned and cut in
    1-inch pieces
1 medium green pepper, seeded and
    cut in 1-inch pieces
1 large onion, peeled and quartered
1 teaspoon cumin
1 can (28 ounces) whole tomatoes,
    drained
1 cup pimento-stuffed olives
1 can (8 ounces) corn, drained

1. In a paper bag, dredge chicken in flour, salt, and pepper.
2. In a large skillet, brown chicken on both sides in butter and oil and remove from pan.
3. Using **steel blade,** separately process garlic until minced; carrot, celery, green pepper, and onion until finely chopped. Add to the skillet in which chicken was browned, sauté for about 5 minutes, and remove from pan.
4. Still using **steel blade,** process drained tomatoes until finely chopped.
5. Place chicken in a large Dutch oven or covered casserole. Add cooked chopped vegetables, sprinkle with cumin, and top with chopped tomatoes. Cover Dutch oven.
6. Bake at 350°F 45 minutes.
7. Using **slicing disc,** slice olives. Add sliced olives and corn and cook 15 minutes longer, or until chicken is tender. Serve with **rice.**

*6 servings*

# Sweet and Sour Chicken

*Sauce:*
¾ cup chicken stock
¼ cup brown sugar
¼ cup sugar
½ cup vinegar
¼ cup ketchup
1 tablespoon sherry
1 tablespoon cornstarch
2 tablespoons soy sauce
¼ cup pineapple juice

*Chicken:*
1 chicken breast, boned, skinned,
    and partially frozen
1 clove garlic
2 slices fresh ginger, each slice cut in
    quarters (1 teaspoon minced)
3 tablespoons peanut oil
1 green pepper, cut in 1-inch pieces
1 tomato, cut in 1-inch pieces
½ cup pineapple chunks, drained
    (reserving liquid)

1. For sauce, combine stock, sugars, vinegar, ketchup, and sherry in a saucepan. Bring to a boil, stirring to dissolve sugar.
2. Blend cornstarch, soy sauce, and pineapple juice. Stir into mixture in saucepan and cook over low heat until thickened.
3. For chicken, using **slicing disc,** slice meat (page 13). Set aside.
4. Using **steel blade,** mince garlic and ginger root by starting machine and adding ingredients through feed tube. Set aside.
5. Heat 2 tablespoons peanut oil in a wok. Add minced garlic and ginger root and stir-fry a few seconds. Add sliced chicken and stir-fry until just tender. Remove from pan and set aside.
6. Heat 1 tablespoon peanut oil in wok and stir-fry green peppers 2 to 3 minutes. Add tomato, pineapple, and chicken and stir-fry only to heat through.
7. Remove to a serving dish and spoon sauce over the top. Serve at once with **rice.**

*4 servings*

# Chicken Paprikash

3 pounds chicken, cut in serving
  pieces
  Flour for dredging
4 tablespoons butter
1 tablespoon oil
¼ cup fresh parsley, cleaned and
  trimmed (2 tablespoons chopped)
1 clove garlic
1 large carrot, pared and cut in
  1-inch pieces
1 stalk celery, cut in 1-inch pieces
2 large onions, peeled and quartered
3 tablespoons flour
1 tablespoon paprika
2 cups chicken stock
¼ pound mushrooms, cleaned and
  trimmed
½ cup dairy sour cream

1. Dredge chicken in flour. In a large skillet, brown chicken on both sides in 2 tablespoons butter and 1 tablespoon oil.
2. Meanwhile, using **steel blade,** separately process parsley until chopped, garlic until minced, carrot and celery together until finely chopped, and onions until coarsely chopped. Remove each from bowl and set aside.
3. After chicken has browned, remove from skillet and set aside. Heat remaining butter in same skillet and sauté chopped vegetables and parsley until tender. Stir in flour and paprika. Gradually add stock, stirring with a whisk until smooth. Simmer about 5 minutes.
4. Using **steel blade,** process vegetable mixture until puréed and return to skillet.
5. Using **slicing disc,** slice mushrooms and add to purée. Also return browned chicken pieces to skillet.
6. Cover and simmer until chicken is tender (45 minutes to 1 hour).
7. Remove chicken, stir in sour cream, and return chicken. Heat thoroughly without boiling. Adjust seasonings. Serve with **Spätzle** (page 32).

*6 servings*

# Ravioli with Cheese, Spinach, or Chicken Filling

**Pasta:**
  2 eggs
  2 cups semolina flour
  ¾ teaspoon salt
  1 teaspoon olive oil
  ¼ cup warm water

  Cheese, Spinach, or Chicken
    Filling
  Tomato Sauce (page 39) or Cream
    Sauce (page 39)

1. For pasta, using **steel blade,** lightly beat eggs. Add flour, salt, and olive oil and process a few seconds. With machine on, add water through the feed tube and process until dough forms into a ball.
2. Remove dough from bowl, cover it with a damp towel and let it rest for 30 minutes.
3. Divide the dough in half. Roll out dough on a lightly floured board to a thickness about that of a dime. Using a cookie cutter or a ravioli press, cut dough into 2-inch ravioli shapes. Fill with 1 heaping teaspoon filling mixture and seal ravioli. Put ravioli on a lightly floured towel and cover with a towel. Let dry at least 1½ hours before cooking.
4. Cook ravioli in a large pot of boiling water 15 to 20 minutes, or until done. Remove with a slotted spoon. Place in a well-heated serving dish and spoon sauce over them. Toss lightly, sprinkle with **grated Parmesan cheese,** and serve immediately.

*About 40 (2-inch) ravioli*

## Cheese Filling

1 cube (1 inch) Parmesan cheese (2
  tablespoons grated)

Using **steel blade,** separately process Parmesan cheese to a fine powder and parsley until chopped. Return both to bowl.

2 tablespoons fresh parsley, cleaned and trimmed (1 tablespoon chopped)
¾ pound ricotta cheese, drained
1 egg yolk
½ teaspoon sugar
⅛ teaspoon salt
  Pinch nutmeg

Add remaining ingredients and process until thoroughly blended.

*Enough filling for 40 ravioli*

## Spinach Filling

1 pound spinach, washed and trimmed
1 cube (1 inch) Parmesan cheese (2 tablespoons grated)
½ pound ricotta cheese, drained
1 tablespoon butter
1 egg yolk
¼ teaspoon salt
¼ teaspoon pepper
  Pinch nutmeg

1. Cook the spinach in the water that clings to the leaves for 10 minutes, covered, over medium heat. Drain it thoroughly by hand-squeezing it.
2. Using **steel blade,** process Parmesan cheese to a fine powder. Add drained spinach and remaining ingredients to the bowl and process until thoroughly blended and of a pastelike consistency.

*Enough filling for 40 ravioli*

## Chicken Filling

1 boneless chicken breast
2 tablespoons butter
1 cube (1 inch) Parmesan cheese (2 tablespoons grated)
½ pound ricotta cheese, drained
2 egg yolks
½ teaspoon grated lemon peel
⅛ teaspoon nutmeg
¼ teaspoon salt
⅛ teaspoon pepper

1. Cook chicken breast in butter until it is cooked through and tender. Cut in 1-inch pieces.
2. Using **steel blade,** process Parmesan cheese to a fine powder. Add chicken and process until finely chopped. Add remaining ingredients and process until thoroughly blended and of a pastelike consistency.

*Enough filling for 40 ravioli*

## Tomato Sauce

1 can (28 ounces) tomatoes
1 can (6 ounces) tomato paste
1 cup water
¼ cup olive oil
1 clove garlic
¼ cup butter
1 teaspoon sugar
½ teaspoon salt
¼ teaspoon pepper
¼ teaspoon basil

1. Strain tomatoes and reserve liquid. Using **steel blade,** add tomatoes to the bowl and process until finely chopped.
2. Put chopped tomatoes into a saucepan; add liquid, tomato paste, water, oil, and garlic. Simmer for 20 minutes.
3. Remove garlic. Add butter, sugar, salt, pepper, and basil and simmer 20 minutes longer.

## Cream Sauce

8 cubes (1 inch each) Parmesan cheese (1 cup grated)
1 cup whipping cream
8 tablespoons butter

1. Using **steel blade,** process Parmesan cheese to a fine powder.
2. In a saucepan, combine cream and butter and cook over low heat until butter is melted. Add half of Parmesan cheese and stir until cheese is melted.
3. Pour sauce over cooked and drained ravioli and toss gently. Sprinkle with remaining Parmesan cheese and serve immediately.

# Veal Chops with Onion-Cheese Sauce

6 **large veal chops**
**Milk**
4 **cubes (1 inch each) Parmesan**
   **cheese (½ cup grated)**
2 **ounces Swiss cheese (1 cup**
   **shredded)**
4 **large onions, peeled and quartered**
   **Butter (about ⅔ cup)**
   **Flour**
2 **tablespoons oil**
½ **teaspoon salt**
¼ **teaspoon pepper**

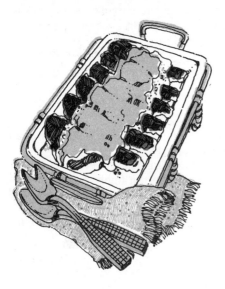

1. Cover veal with milk and soak for 1 hour.
2. Using **steel blade,** process Parmesan cheese to a fine powder and set aside.
3. Using **shredding disc,** shred Swiss cheese and set aside.
4. Using **steel blade,** process onions, one at a time with quick on/off motions, until finely chopped. In a large skillet, sauté onion in 4 tablespoons butter for about 5 minutes. Cover and steam onion over low heat until transparent and tender, but not browned.
5. Remove chops from milk, reserving milk in a 2-cup measure. Dry on a paper towel, then dust lightly with flour. In a separate skillet, heat 4 tablespoons butter and the oil and brown chops on both sides.
6. Lower the heat, and cook until chops are tender, turning once. Place cooked veal chops in a flat baking dish and keep warm.
7. Meanwhile, drain cooked onion and add liquid to the reserved milk. Add milk, if necessary, to fill to the 1½-cup line.
8. To the skillet in which veal chops were cooked, add enough butter to make 3 tablespoons fat. Add ¼ cup flour, stirring constantly, and cook for about 3 minutes. Slowly add milk-onion mixture, stirring with a wire whisk until smooth and thickened. Add salt, pepper, and Parmesan cheese and cook until thoroughly blended and cheese has melted.
9. Top each veal chop with some of the drained steamed onion. Pour sauce over all and sprinkle with shredded Swiss cheese.
10. Heat in a 475°F oven until cheese melts and browns lightly.

*6 servings*

# Lamb Leg on a Bed of Spinach

*Lamb:*
1 **lamb leg (6 pounds)**
4 **cloves garlic**
2 **carrots, pared and cut in 1-inch**
   **pieces**
2 **stalks celery, trimmed and cut in**
   **1-inch pieces**
1 **large onion, peeled and quartered**
2 **tablespoons fresh parsley, cleaned**
   **and trimmed (1 tablespoon**
   **chopped)**
⅛ **teaspoon each thyme, oregano,**
   **savory, and basil**
1 **cup beef stock**

*Spinach:*
3 **pounds spinach, cleaned and**
   **trimmed**

1. For lamb, put lamb in a roasting pan and stud with 2 cloves garlic, cut in slivers. Bake at 400°F 15 minutes to brown.
2. Meanwhile, using **steel blade,** process remaining garlic, carrots, celery, onion, and parsley all together until finely chopped.
3. After meat has browned, remove from pan. Turn oven down to 350°F. Add chopped vegetables, spices, and beef stock to roasting pan. Place lamb on top. Cover tightly and return to oven. Roast 20 to 25 minutes per pound.

4. For spinach, put spinach into a saucepan with just the water that clings to the leaves, sprinkle with salt, and cook until almost tender (8 to 10 minutes). Remove to a colander and immediately rinse with cold water. Take the spinach in handfuls and squeeze out as much water as possible.
5. Using **steel blade** and working with small batches, process the spinach, using quick on/off motions, until chopped.
6. In an enameled pan, heat 2 tablespoons butter and add

1 teaspoon salt
6 tablespoons butter
⅛ teaspoon pepper
Pinch nutmeg

# Lamb Curry

1 lamb leg (4 to 5 pounds)
4 tablespoons butter
2 cloves garlic
2 stalks celery, trimmed and cut in
    1-inch pieces
2 apples, pared, cored, and
    quartered
2 carrots, pared and cut in 1-inch
    pieces
2 onions, peeled and quartered
2 ripe bananas, peeled and cut in
    1-inch pieces
1 can (16 ounces) tomatoes
1 tablespoon curry powder
2 tablespoons flour
1 cup chicken stock
½ teaspoon salt
¼ teaspoon pepper
    Saffron Rice

## Saffron Rice

2 cups uncooked rice
5 cups water
6 tablespoons butter
2 teaspoons salt
    Pinch saffron

chopped spinach. Cook over high heat 2 to 3 minutes, stirring constantly, until moisture has cooked away.

7. Add remaining butter, pepper, and nutmeg. Cover and cook slowly 10 minutes until butter is absorbed and spinach is tender. Season with more salt and pepper if necessary.

8. To assemble, remove lamb from roasting pan. Let it stand at room temperature for about 15 minutes. Remove fat and strain sauce, reserving liquid. Using **steel blade**, process vegetable mixture until puréed. With machine running, add strained liquid through the feed tube. Return sauce to pan and simmer.

9. Spread spinach on a serving dish and keep warm.

10. Carve lamb into thin slices and overlap them on the bed of spinach. Serve the sauce separately.

*8 servings*

1. Bone and trim lamb of fat. Cut into 1-inch cubes. Heat butter in a Dutch oven and sauté lamb until no longer pink.

2. Using **steel blade**, mince garlic. Separately process celery, apples, carrots, onions, and bananas until finely chopped; set aside. Drain tomatoes, reserving juice, and chop until fine.

3. Add the chopped ingredients, except tomatoes, to lamb. Sprinkle with curry powder and flour and stir until meat is coated. Add the chopped tomatoes, tomato juice, chicken stock, salt, and pepper; cover.

4. Bake at 375°F 1½ hours, or until meat is tender.

5. Serve with Saffron Rice and condiments.

*8 servings*

Put all ingredients into a saucepan and bring to a boil. Stir, cover, and let simmer 20 to 30 minutes, or until rice is tender.

## Suggested Condiments

Using **steel blade:**
  — grated fresh coconut
  — chopped crisp bacon
  — chopped hard-cooked eggs (yolks and whites chopped separately)
  — chopped peanuts or cashews
  — chopped tomatoes
  — chopped cucumbers

Using **slicing disc:**
  — sliced red and green peppers
  — sliced green onions
  — sliced bananas sautéed in butter

Other:
  — raisins or currants soaked in sherry
  — grapefruit sections soaked in sherry

*Make with cucumber soup (James Beard, Cuisinart) + Greek Salad (p. 67 here)*
*use my 13 × 8 = French white baking dish — makes really*
*6–8 servings (dep. on what else served)*

# Moussaka

*Very good ✓*

*Tastes better with less of a cheese topping.*

- 4 slices dry bread, cut in quarters (1 cup crumbs)
- 8 cubes (1 inch each) Parmesan cheese (1 cup grated)
- 1 cup fresh parsley, cleaned and trimmed (½ cup chopped)
- 3 medium onions, peeled and quartered
- 8 tablespoons butter (1 stick)
- 1 pound lamb, cut in 1-inch cubes
- 1 pound beef, cut in 1-inch cubes
- 2 large eggplant, pared  *3 at least*
- 1 can (6 ounces) tomato paste
- 1 can (8 ounces) tomato sauce
- ½ cup red wine
- ½ teaspoon cinnamon
- ½ teaspoon salt
- ¼ teaspoon pepper

**Cheese Sauce:**

*For my 13 × 8 = dish need only ½ of this sauce max.*

- 8 tablespoons butter (1 stick)
- 6 tablespoons flour
- 1 quart milk, heated
- 4 eggs
- 2 cups cottage cheese
- ½ teaspoon nutmeg  *½–¼*

1. Using **steel blade,** separately process bread to fine crumbs, Parmesan cheese to a fine powder, parsley and onions until chopped. Remove each from bowl and set aside. In a saucepan, cook chopped onion in 4 tablespoons butter until tender.
2. Still using **steel blade,** process meat in ½-pound batches until finely chopped. Add chopped meat to onion and cook 10 minutes longer.
3. Meanwhile, cut pared eggplant into lengthwise quarters to fit feed tube. Slice with **slicing disc.** In a covered skillet, cook eggplant in 4 tablespoons butter until tender.
4. Add tomato paste, tomato sauce, wine, chopped parsley, cinnamon, salt, and pepper to onion-meat mixture. Simmer 10 minutes and remove from heat.
5. Using **steel blade,** lightly beat eggs and set aside.
6. To make Cheese Sauce, melt butter in a saucepan, add flour, and cook 2 minutes, stirring constantly. Gradually add hot milk, stirring until thickened and smooth. Remove from heat, cool slightly, and stir in beaten eggs, cottage cheese, and nutmeg.
7. Butter a 14×10-inch baking pan and sprinkle lightly with bread crumbs. Arrange alternate layers of meat sauce and eggplant, sprinkling each layer with bread crumbs and Parmesan cheese.
8. Pour Cheese Sauce over top.
9. Bake at 375°F 1 hour, or until top is golden. Remove from oven and cool 15 minutes before serving.

*12 servings*

*Note:* The flavor of this dish improves on standing one day. Reheat at 350°F 1 hour before serving. *Yes!*

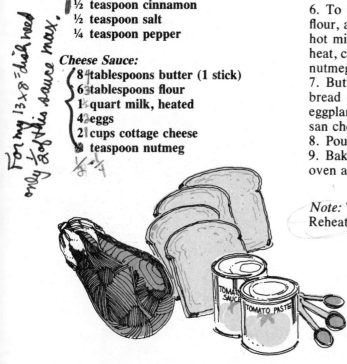

# Shrimp Jambalaya

- ½ cup fresh parsley, cleaned and trimmed (¼ cup chopped)
- 2 cloves garlic
- 1 medium onion, peeled and quartered
- 3 green onions, trimmed and cut in 1-inch pieces
- 1½ medium green peppers, trimmed and cut in 1-inch pieces
- 3 stalks celery, trimmed and cut in 1-inch pieces
- ¼ pound ham, cut in 1-inch cubes

1. Using **steel blade,** separately process parsley, garlic, onion, green onions, 1 green pepper, and celery until finely chopped; and ham until coarsely chopped.
2. In a large heavy skillet, heat butter and cook the chopped ingredients about 5 minutes, or until onion is tender, stirring occasionally.
3. Stir in chicken stock, pepper, thyme, cayenne pepper, and bay leaf. Cover and bring to boiling.
4. Add rice gradually, stirring with a fork. Simmer, covered, 20 minutes, or until rice is tender.
5. Using **steel blade,** process remaining ½ green pepper until coarsely chopped. By hand, coarsely chop tomatoes. Add

3 tablespoons butter
2 cups chicken stock
⅛ teaspoon pepper
¼ teaspoon thyme
⅛ teaspoon cayenne pepper
1 bay leaf
1 cup uncooked rice
1 pound fresh cooked shrimp
3 large fresh tomatoes

chopped pepper, chopped tomatoes, and cooked shrimp. Simmer, uncovered, for about 5 minutes longer.

*6 to 8 servings*

# Fish Mold with Cucumber Sauce

*Stock:*

1 medium carrot, pared and cut in 3½-inch pieces
1 small onion, peeled
¼ cup fresh parsley, cleaned and trimmed
1 bay leaf
4 peppercorns
1½ pounds halibut, whitefish, or pike fillets

*Mold:*

5 slices fresh white bread
(2½ cups crumbs)
½ cup milk
¼ cup fresh parsley, cleaned, and trimmed (2 tablespoons chopped)
½ small onion, peeled and cut in half
¼ pound mushrooms, cleaned and trimmed
3 eggs
4 tablespoons butter, melted
½ cup whipping cream
1 tablespoon lemon juice
1 teaspoon salt
⅛ teaspoon pepper
Pimento strips
Green pepper rings

*Cucumber Sauce:*

2 large cucumbers, pared
1 pint dairy sour cream
1 tablespoon prepared horseradish (or freshly grated to taste)
½ teaspoon salt
¼ teaspoon pepper

1. For stock, using **slicing disc,** slice carrot and onion.
2. Put carrot, onion, parsley, bay leaf, and peppercorns in a large saucepan with enough water to cover vegetables and fish when added. Bring to boiling.
3. Tie fish in a piece of cheesecloth and lower into boiling water. Reduce heat and simmer until fish is tender and flakes easily (about 10 minutes). Remove fish, drain, and flake, discarding bones and skin. Set fish aside.

4. For mold, using **steel blade,** process bread to fine crumbs. Soak bread crumbs with milk in a bowl.
5. Still using **steel blade,** separately process parsley, onion, and mushrooms until finely chopped and remove from bowl.
6. Using **plastic blade,** add eggs to bowl and beat lightly. Add next 5 ingredients together with flaked fish, soaked bread crumbs, chopped parsley, onion, and mushrooms. Process, using quick on/off motions, until thoroughly blended.
7. Generously butter a 5-cup fish or ring mold. Arrange pimento strips and green pepper rings in a pattern on bottom of mold. Turn fish mixture into mold and set in a pan of hot water.
8. Bake at 350°F 1 hour, or until a knife inserted in the center comes out clean.

9. For Cucumber Sauce, slice cucumber in half lengthwise and scoop out seeds. Cut into 3½-inch pieces and shred with **shredding disc.** Drain well in a colander.
10. Using **plastic blade,** add sour cream, horseradish sauce, salt, pepper, and shredded cucumbers to bowl and process, using quick on/off motions, until thoroughly blended. Chill before serving.
11. When ready to serve, turn mold out on a serving plate and surround with **fresh parsley sprigs** and **radish roses.** Serve warm or cold with Cucumber Sauce.

*6 to 8 servings*

# Baked Sole in Champagne

2 ounces Swiss cheese (1 cup shredded)
¼ cup fresh parsley, cleaned and trimmed (2 tablespoons chopped)
1 small onion, peeled and quartered
¼ pound fresh mushrooms, washed and trimmed
1 cup champagne
2 tablespoons butter
1 bay leaf
¼ cup whipping cream
4 sole fillets
Salt and pepper

1. Using **shredding disc,** shred Swiss cheese and set aside.
2. Using **steel blade,** separately process parsley until chopped, and onion until finely chopped. Set aside.
3. Using **slicing disc,** slice mushrooms.
4. In a saucepan, combine champagne, butter, bay leaf, parsley, onion, and mushrooms. Bring to boiling, reduce heat, and cook slowly until reduced by half. Remove bay leaf and mix in cream. Remove from heat.
5. Sprinkle sole fillets with salt and pepper. Place in a baking dish and pour sauce over them. Sprinkle with shredded cheese.
6. Bake at 350°F 25 minutes, or until fish is tender and top is lightly browned.

*4 servings*

# Russian Salmon Mound

*Pastry:*
4 cups flour
2 sticks butter, frozen and cut in 12 pieces
6 tablespoons shortening
1 teaspoon salt
12 tablespoons ice water

*Salmon:*
3 quarts water
2 cups dry white wine
1 large onion, peeled and quartered
2 stalks celery, trimmed and cut in 1-inch pieces
2 carrots, pared and cut in 1-inch pieces
10 peppercorns
1 tablespoon salt
2½ pounds fresh salmon

*Mushroom-Rice Filling:*
8 tablespoons butter (1 stick)
½ cup uncooked rice
1¼ cups chicken stock
1 tablespoon dried dill
½ pound fresh mushrooms, cleaned and trimmed
3 tablespoons lemon juice
3 large onions, peeled and quartered
1½ teaspoons salt
¼ teaspoon pepper
3 hard-cooked eggs

1. To make pastry, using **steel blade,** place 2 cups flour, 1 stick butter cut in 6 pieces, 3 tablespoons vegetable shortening, and ½ teaspoon salt in bowl. Process until butter and shortening are cut into flour. With machine on, add 6 tablespoons ice water through feed tube. Process until dough forms into a ball and remove from bowl.
2. Repeat procedure again, using same amounts of ingredients. Wrap both balls of dough in plastic wrap and place in refrigerator to chill while preparing remainder of recipe.

3. To cook salmon, combine 3 quarts water and wine in a large pot.
4. Using **steel blade,** chop onion, celery, and carrots together. Add to pot. Also add peppercorns and salt. Bring to boiling over high heat. Add salmon to liquid, reduce heat, and simmer for about 10 minutes until tender. Remove from pot and separate into small flakes with a fork. Also remove any bones and skin from fish. Set aside.

5. To make filling, melt 2 tablespoons butter in a saucepan, add rice and cook 2 to 3 minutes until rice is coated with butter. Add chicken stock, bring to a boil, and cover. Reduce heat and cook about 20 minutes until tender and fluffy. Remove from heat and stir in dill with a fork. Set aside.
6. Slice mushrooms with **slicing disc.** Melt 2 tablespoons butter in a skillet, add mushrooms, and cook for 5 minutes. Transfer to a small bowl and toss with lemon juice; set aside.
7. Using **steel blade,** process onions until chopped. Melt 4 tablespoons butter in skillet, add chopped onion, and cook until soft, but not brown. Add mushrooms, salt, and pepper; set aside.
8. Using **plastic blade,** process hard-cooked eggs until finely chopped and set aside.

9. To make Cream Sauce, melt 2 tablespoons butter and add

*Cream Sauce:*
- 2 **tablespoons butter**
- 3½ **tablespoons flour**
- 2 **cups milk, heated**
- ¼ **teaspoon salt**
- **Dash pepper**

*Assembly:*
- 2 **tablespoons soft butter**
- 1 **egg yolk**
- 1 **tablespoon cream**
- 1 **tablespoon melted butter**

flour. Cook for a minute or two, remove from heat and add heated milk, stirring constantly with a whisk until smooth. Bring to boiling, add salt and pepper, and remove from heat.

10. In a large bowl, combine flaked salmon, mushroom-onion mixture, rice, chopped hard-cooked eggs, and Cream Sauce. Gently toss with two wooden spoons until thoroughly mixed. Adjust seasonings, adding more salt, pepper, and dill as desired.

11. To assemble, roll 1 ball of dough into a rectangle and trim to 15×8 inches. Coat a large cookie sheet with 2 tablespoons butter. Drape pastry around rolling pin and unroll over cookie sheet. Place filling in center, forming it into a mound and leaving a 2-inch border around edges. Using a pastry brush, coat border with a mixture of 1 egg yolk and 1 tablespoon cream.

12. Roll other ball of dough into a rectangle 18×11 inches. Roll it around rolling pin and place over salmon mound. Trim borders of dough so that they are even. Turn up border of dough to make a shallow rim around mound and decorate (crimp) at ½-inch intervals with dull side of a knife. Cut a 1-inch circle in center of mound and decorate top with leftover pastry. Brush entire loaf with egg yolk mixture. Pour 1 tablespoon melted butter in opening.

13. Bake at 400°F 1 hour, or until golden. Serve with a pitcher of **melted butter** or bowl of **dairy sour cream.**

*12 servings*

# Stuffed Butterfly Shrimp

- 12 **jumbo shrimp**
- 8 **whole saltines, broken in quarters**
- 2 **cubes (1 inch each) Parmesan cheese (¼ cup grated)**
- ¼ **cup fresh parsley, cleaned and trimmed (2 tablespoons chopped)**
- 1 **hard-cooked egg**
- 1 **clove garlic**
- 1 **medium onion, peeled and quartered**
- 6 **tablespoons butter**
- ¼ **teaspoon thyme**
- ¼ **teaspoon tarragon**
- ¼ **teaspoon pepper**
- 2 **ounces mushrooms**
- ½ **cup cream**

1. To prepare butterfly shrimp, cut almost through each shrimp lengthwise and remove sand vein. Rinse, then drain on paper towels.

2. Using **steel blade,** separately process crackers to fine crumbs, Parmesan cheese to a fine powder, parsley until chopped, and hard-cooked egg until finely chopped. Remove each from bowl and set aside.

3. Still using **steel blade,** mince garlic. Add onion and process until chopped.

4. In a skillet, melt 3 tablespoons butter. Add onion, garlic, parsley, thyme, tarragon, and pepper and sauté until onion is lightly browned.

5. Using **steel blade,** process mushrooms, using quick on/off motions, until finely chopped. Add to skillet and cook a few minutes. Add chopped hard-cooked egg and cook a couple minutes more. Remove from heat.

6. With **plastic blade** in bowl, combine mushroom mixture with cracker crumbs and cream; process, with quick on/off motions, until blended.

7. Pile filling onto each flattened shrimp. Sprinkle with Parmesan cheese. Melt remaining 3 tablespoons butter and pour over shrimp.

8. Place on lowest rack of broiler and broil until stuffing is golden brown and shrimp are tender.

*4 servings*

# Stuffed Cabbage

1 **large head cabbage**
¼ **cup fresh parsley, cleaned and trimmed (2 tablespoons chopped)**
1 **carrot, pared and cut in 1-inch pieces**
½ **medium onion, peeled and cut in half**
2 **pounds beef, cut in 1-inch cubes**
2 **eggs**
⅔ **cup cooked rice**
1 **teaspoon salt**
½ **teaspoon pepper**
¼ **cup cider vinegar**
½ **cup firmly packed brown sugar**
1 **can (15 ounces) tomato sauce**
1 **can (6 ounces) tomato paste**
1 **can (16 ounces) tomatoes**

1. Core the head of cabbage and place in a pot of boiling water for a few minutes. When outer leaves start to wilt and separate easily, remove from water to a colander and remove as many leaves as possible, being careful not to tear them. Return cabbage to pot and repeat until most leaves have been removed.

2. Using **steel blade,** process leftover center of cabbage, using quick on/off motions, until coarsely chopped. Set aside.

3. With a sharp knife, trim off the tough rib from the back of each cabbage leaf. Set leaves aside.

4. Using **steel blade,** process parsley until chopped and set aside. Add carrot and onion, and process together until finely chopped; remove from bowl.

5. Using **steel blade,** process meat in ½-pound batches until finely chopped and set aside.

6. With **plastic blade** in the bowl, add half of meat and half of carrot-onion mixture. To this mixture, add 1 egg, ⅓ cup cooked rice, ½ teaspoon salt, ¼ teaspoon pepper, and 1 tablespoon parsley. Process, using quick on/off motions, until blended. Remove from bowl and repeat, using remaining half of ingredients.

7. Nestle a ball of meat the size of a small plum at the base of each cabbage leaf; fold in sides and tightly roll cabbage around meat. If any meat is left over, shape into 1-inch balls and set aside.

8. In a large deep skillet or Dutch oven, put vinegar, brown sugar, tomato sauce, tomato paste, and reserved chopped cabbage.

9. Drain can of tomatoes, adding juice to skillet. Using **steel blade,** process tomatoes until finely chopped and add to skillet.

10. Gently place cabbage rolls in skillet mixture. Add meatballs. Cover and simmer about 2 hours.

*About 20 cabbage rolls*

# LUNCH AND BRUNCH DISHES

# Shrimp Pancakes with Cheese Sauce

**Pancakes:**
- 8 cubes (1 inch each) Parmesan cheese (1 cup grated)
- ½ pound fresh shrimp, shelled and cooked
- 2 eggs
- ¾ cup flour
- 1 cup cream
- 5 tablespoons milk
- 1 tablespoon butter, melted
- ¼ teaspoon salt

**Cheese Sauce:**
- 3 ounces sharp Cheddar cheese (1½ cups shredded)
- 3 tablespoons butter
- 3 tablespoons flour
- 2½ cups milk, scalded
- ¼ teaspoon salt
- ⅛ teaspoon nutmeg

1. For pancakes, using **steel blade,** process Parmesan cheese to a fine powder. Set aside.
2. Using **steel blade,** process cooked shrimp until finely chopped. Set aside.
3. Using **steel blade,** add eggs to bowl and beat lightly. Add remaining ingredients for pancakes and ½ cup grated Parmesan cheese and process until thoroughly blended.
4. In a hot well-buttered 8-inch skillet (crêpe or omelet), drop 3 tablespoons batter. Tilt pan to spread batter evenly into a 6-inch pancake. Fry until lightly browned. Turn and brown other side. Remove to a platter, cool about 1 minute, then roll up and place on a serving dish.
5. Before cooking next pancake, add 1 teaspoon melted butter to the skillet to coat bottom, and pour off excess. Cook next pancake and repeat process until all batter is used up.
6. Sprinkle rolled pancakes generously with remaining Parmesan cheese and keep them hot in a 250°F oven.

7. For sauce, using **shredding disc,** shred cheese and set aside.
8. In a saucepan, melt butter, gradually stir in flour, and cook 2 to 3 minutes. Slowly stir in milk, and continue to cook, stirring with a whisk until sauce is thickened and smooth. Add shredded cheese, salt, and nutmeg and stir until cheese is melted.
9. Serve Cheese Sauce on the side.

*15 (6-inch) pancakes;*
*3 cups Cheese Sauce*

# Feta Cheese Strudel

- 2 slices dry bread (½ cup crumbs)
- ½ cup fresh parsley, cleaned and trimmed (¼ cup chopped)
- 3 green onions, cut in 1-inch pieces
- 3 eggs
- ½ pound feta cheese
- 1 cup cottage cheese
  Dash nutmeg
- 1 pound filo pastry sheets
- 8 tablespoons butter, melted

1. Using **steel blade,** separately process bread to fine crumbs and parsley and green onions until chopped. Set aside.
2. Using **steel blade,** lightly beat eggs. Add cheeses, nutmeg, chopped parsley, and green onions; process, using quick on/off motions, until thoroughly blended.
3. Unroll filo sheets and keep covered with a damp cloth while working, since they dry out very quickly. On another damp towel place 1 filo sheet. Brush with melted butter and lightly sprinkle with bread crumbs. Place another sheet on top, brush with butter, and sprinkle with bread crumbs. Repeat, using 10 sheets in all.
4. Spoon half of the cheese mixture evenly on the pastry sheet to within 1 inch of short sides and 3 inches of long sides. Fold long side up over filling, then brush with butter. Fold short sides in and roll the long side over in jelly-roll fashion. Be sure to roll tightly. Place seam side down on a buttered baking sheet. Brush again with butter.
5. Repeat procedure for another roll.
6. Bake at 375°F 35 to 40 minutes, or until golden brown.

*About 20 servings*

*Note:* Any leftover filo sheets can be refrozen.
   If desired for easier cutting, before baking make cuts 1 inch apart about two thirds of the way through rolls.

# Sour Cream Blintzes

**Blintzes:**
- 1 egg
- ¾ cup dairy sour cream
- ¾ cup milk
- ⅛ teaspoon salt
- 1 teaspoon sugar
- 1 cup flour
- 1 tablespoon butter, melted

**Filling:**
- 1 carton (8 ounces) cottage cheese
- 1 package (8 ounces) cream cheese, cut in quarters
- 1 egg
- 2 tablespoons butter, melted
- 2 tablespoons sugar
- 1 teaspoon vanilla extract
- ¼ cup golden raisins (optional)

**Apricot Sauce:**
- 1 pound dried apricots
- ¾ cup sugar
- Orange liqueur (optional)

1. For blintzes, using **steel blade,** add egg, sour cream, milk, salt, and sugar to bowl. Process until light and fluffy. Add flour and butter and process until smooth.

2. Drop 2 tablespoons batter into a hot buttered 8-inch omelet or crêpe pan. Tilt pan to spread batter evenly into a 5-inch circle. Cook until light golden brown. Turn and cook other side briefly but do not brown. Repeat process until all batter is used. Remember to butter pan before each blintz is cooked and pour off excess butter.

3. Stack blintzes, browned side up, on a plate and cover with a dome-type cover to prevent them from drying out.

4. For filling, using **steel blade,** place all ingredients, except raisins, in the bowl and process until smooth and creamy. Add raisins, if desired, and process, with quick on/off motions, until blended.

5. Place a heaping tablespoon of cheese filling on each pancake. Tuck in opposite sides and roll up.

6. Arrange rolled pancakes in a buttered baking dish.

7. Set in a 350°F oven 10 to 15 minutes, or until heated through.

8. For Apricot Sauce, cover apricots with water and cook until soft. Drain, reserving juice.

9. Using **steel blade,** process until puréed, adding additional strained juice to reach desired consistency. Add sugar and process until sugar is blended into sauce. Return to saucepan and heat thoroughly. Sauce can be flavored with orange liqueur, if desired.

10. Serve with blintzes and **sour cream.**

# Cynthia's Cottage Cheese Pancakes

- 6 eggs, separated
- 2 cups cottage cheese
- 2 tablespoons sugar
- ½ teaspoon salt
- ⅔ cup flour
- Pinch cinnamon and nutmeg
- ⅛ teaspoon cream of tartar

1. Using **plastic blade,** process egg yolks, cottage cheese, sugar, salt, flour, cinnamon, and nutmeg until thoroughly blended.

2. Using a mixer, beat egg whites in a large bowl with cream of tartar until stiff, but not dry, peaks are formed. Gently add egg-yolk mixture to bowl and fold together.

3. Drop batter by large spoonfuls to make 4-inch pancakes on an oiled skillet or griddle. Fry until golden on both sides and puffy.

4. Sprinkle with confectioners' sugar and serve with sour cream, preserves, honey, or applesauce on the side.

*About 30 (4-inch) pancakes*

# German Apple Pancakes

3 small apples, pared, cored, and
    quartered
10 tablespoons butter
3 tablespoons sugar
1 teaspoon cinnamon
4 eggs
⅓ cup milk
¼ cup flour
¼ teaspoon salt
    Confectioners' sugar

1. Using **slicing disc,** slice apples. Heat 4 tablespoons butter in a 10-inch skillet. Add apple slices, cover, and cook over medium heat until apples are almost tender, gently turning slices several times during cooking. When almost tender, sprinkle a mixture of 2 tablespoons sugar and the cinnamon evenly over the apples. Continue cooking, uncovered, until apples are just tender. Turn into a bowl and keep warm.

2. Using **plastic blade,** beat eggs thoroughly and blend in milk. Add flour, 1 tablespoon sugar, and salt and process a few seconds until blended and smooth.

3. Heat 3 tablespoons of the butter in the skillet until moderately hot. Pour in enough batter to cover bottom of skillet. Spoon about one half of the apple mixture evenly over batter. Pour in just enough batter to cover apples.

4. Bake pancake over medium heat until golden brown on the bottom. Loosen edges with a spatula and carefully turn and brown the other side.

5. When pancake is baked, remove skillet from heat and brush pancake generously with melted butter. Roll up and transfer to a warm serving platter. Sift confectioners' sugar over the top. Keep pancake hot. Repeat procedure with remaining batter and apples.

*2 apple pancakes*

# Mushroom-Tarragon Eggs Mornay

**Filling:**
1 slice dry bread, cut in quarters
    (¼ cup crumbs)
2 cubes (1 inch each) Parmesan
    cheese (4 tablespoons grated)
¼ cup fresh parsley, cleaned and
    trimmed (2 tablespoons
    chopped)
5 green onions, cleaned, trimmed,
    and cut in 2-inch pieces
2 tablespoons butter
½ pound fresh mushrooms, cleaned
    and trimmed
1 teaspoon lemon juice
6 hard-cooked eggs

1. For filling, using **steel blade,** separately process bread to fine crumbs, Parmesan cheese to a fine powder, parsley and green onions until finely chopped. Set each aside.

2. In a saucepan, sauté chopped green onions in butter until tender.

3. Using **steel blade,** process mushrooms in 2 batches, using quick on/off motions, until finely chopped. Sprinkle with lemon juice to prevent them from discoloring. Add mushrooms to saucepan and cook until all liquid has evaporated.

4. Cut hard-cooked eggs in half lengthwise and remove yolks.

5. Using **plastic blade,** add egg yolks, mushroom mixture, chopped parsley, 3 tablespoons Parmesan cheese, salt, pepper, and tarragon to the bowl. Process, using quick on/off motions, until blended and of a pastelike consistency.

¼ teaspoon salt
⅛ teaspoon pepper
½ teaspoon tarragon

**Sauce:**
2 ounces Swiss cheese (1 cup shredded)
2 tablespoons butter
3 tablespoons flour
2½ cups milk, heated
½ teaspoon salt
⅛ teaspoon pepper
Pinch nutmeg
2 tablespoons butter, melted

6. Fill the egg whites with the mixture, mounding tops; set aside.
7. For sauce, using **shredding disc,** shred cheese and set aside.
8. In a saucepan, melt butter and stir in flour. Cook 1 to 2 minutes. Gradually add heated milk, stirring with a whisk until thickened and smooth.
9. Add shredded cheese, salt, pepper, and nutmeg and stir over low heat until cheese is melted.
10. Spread a thin layer of cheese sauce into a shallow baking dish. Place filled eggs in dish and pour cheese sauce over top.
11. Combine bread crumbs, remainder of Parmesan cheese, and melted butter; sprinkle a little of mixture over each egg.
12. Bake at 350°F about 10 minutes and place under broiler for a few minutes to brown, if desired.

*6 servings*

# Crêpes Farcie

**Crêpes:**
½ pound fresh spinach, cleaned and trimmed
2 egg yolks
¼ teaspoon salt
Dash pepper
1 cup flour

**Filling:**
3 cubes (1 inch each) Parmesan cheese (6 tablespoons grated cheese)
1 medium onion, peeled and quartered
4 tablespoons butter
2 ounces mushrooms, cleaned and trimmed
1 pound cooked chicken, cut in 1-inch pieces
2 tablespoons flour
1 cup milk
1 tablespoon sherry

**Sauce:**
4 tablespoons butter
4 tablespoons flour
2 cups milk
¾ teaspoon salt
¼ teaspoon pepper
Pinch nutmeg
1 tablespoon sherry
Parmesan cheese

1. For crêpes, cook spinach and drain well. Using **steel blade,** process until finely chopped. Add egg yolks, salt, and pepper and process a few seconds until blended. Add flour and process until dough forms into a ball.
2. On a lightly floured surface, roll out dough ¹/₁₆ inch thick. Cut into 4-inch squares.
3. Add squares one at a time to boiling salted water and cook 4 to 5 minutes, or until tender. Remove with a slotted spoon and cool separately.
4. For filling, using **steel blade,** separately process Parmesan cheese to a fine powder and onion until chopped. In a saucepan, sauté chopped onion in butter until transparent.
5. Using **steel blade,** separately process mushrooms and chicken, using quick on/off motions, until finely chopped. You should have about 1½ cups chopped chicken. Add mushrooms and chicken to saucepan and cook about 5 minutes, stirring occasionally. Add flour and cook 1 or 2 minutes. Gradually add milk, stirring constantly until thickened. Mix in sherry and 2 tablespoons grated Parmesan cheese.
6. Spoon filling along center of each pasta square and roll to form a tube.
7. For sauce, in same saucepan in which chicken was cooked, melt butter and blend in flour. Stir until bubbly. Gradually add milk, stirring with a whisk until smooth. Bring to boiling. Cook and stir 1 to 2 minutes. Mix in salt, pepper, nutmeg, and sherry.
8. Spread a thin layer of sauce in a shallow baking dish. Arrange filled rolls on top and pour cream sauce over all. Sprinkle with remainder of grated Parmesan cheese.
9. Set in a 350°F oven until thoroughly heated.

*4 servings*

# Puffy Omelets with Crab Meat Sauce

**Crab Meat Sauce:**
- 1 small onion, peeled and quartered
- 1 apple, pared, cored, and quartered
- 1 carrot, pared and cut in 1-inch pieces
- 1 stalk celery, trimmed and cut in 1-inch pieces
- 6 tablespoons butter
- 2 cans (7 ounces each) crab meat
- 3 tablespoons flour
- 2 cups milk, heated
- 1 teaspoon grated lemon peel
- 1 tablespoon lemon juice
- ⅛ teaspoon dry mustard
- ½ teaspoon curry powder
- ½ teaspoon salt
- Pinch nutmeg

**Omelets:**
- 8 eggs, separated
- ½ cup milk
- 1 teaspoon baking powder
- ½ teaspoon salt
- 3 tablespoons butter

1. For sauce, using **steel blade,** process onion, apple, carrot, and celery together until finely chopped.
2. In a saucepan, sauté mixture in 3 tablespoons butter for 5 minutes.
3. Drain crab meat, reserving liquid. Go over crab meat carefully, removing any tendons. Measure crab meat liquid and add enough water to make ½ cup liquid. Add to vegetables; cover and simmer 20 minutes, or until tender.
4. Meanwhile, in another saucepan, melt remaining butter, add flour, and cook 2 to 3 minutes. Off heat, add heated milk and stir with a whisk until thickened and smooth. Add vegetable mixture and remaining ingredients, except crab meat. Simmer 10 minutes.
5. Strain sauce and return to saucepan. Add crab meat and heat thoroughly.

6. For omelets, using **plastic blade,** add egg yolks, milk, and baking powder to the bowl. Process until foamy and lemon colored.
7. Using a mixer, beat egg whites with salt until stiff, but not dry, peaks are formed. Gently fold in egg-yolk mixture.
8. Melt butter in a 12-inch skillet. Add egg mixture, cover, and cook over a medium-low heat 12 to 15 minutes, or until firm. Turn upside down on a platter. Top with some of Crab Meat Sauce and cut into wedges. Serve with remaining Crab Meat Sauce on the side.

*6 to 8 servings*

# Broccoli Roll with Mushroom Filling

**Broccoli Roll:**
- 1 pound fresh broccoli, cleaned and trimmed
- 1 slice dry bread, cut in quarters (¼ cup crumbs)
- 4 cubes (1 inch each) Parmesan cheese (½ cup grated)
- 1 small onion, peeled and quartered
- 8 tablespoons butter
- ¾ cup flour
- 1 cup milk, heated
- 4 eggs, separated
- ½ teaspoon salt
- ¼ teaspoon pepper

**Mushroom Filling:**
- 1 pound mushrooms, cleaned and trimmed

1. For roll, cook broccoli until tender. Drain thoroughly. Using **steel blade,** process in two batches until puréed. You should have 1½ cups purée. Set aside.
2. Using steel blade, separately process bread to fine crumbs, Parmesan cheese to a fine powder, and onion until finely chopped. Remove from bowl and set aside.
3. Sauté onion in butter until transparent. Add flour and cook, stirring constantly, until flour is golden. Remove from heat and add warm milk, stirring with a whisk until thickened and smooth. Cool for 5 minutes.
4. Using **steel blade,** put sauce into the bowl, add egg yolks, broccoli purée, salt, pepper, and Parmesan cheese. Process until thoroughly blended and smooth.
5. Using a mixer, beat egg whites until stiff, not dry, peaks are formed. Spoon broccoli mixture over surface of egg whites and gently fold together until just blended.
6. Generously butter a 15×10×1-inch jelly-roll pan. Line it with foil and generously butter foil. Coat it lightly with the

8 tablespoons butter
1 bunch green onions, trimmed and
    cut in 1-inch lengths
3 tablespoons flour
½ cup white wine
½ teaspoon salt
¼ teaspoon pepper
1¼ cups milk, heated
    Pinch nutmeg

bread crumbs, shaking the pan to cover it evenly. Pour broccoli mixture into pan and spread it evenly to a ½-inch depth.

7. Bake at 350°F 25 to 30 minutes, or until it starts to shrink from sides of pan.

8. For filling, using **slicing disc,** slice mushrooms and sauté in 4 tablespoons butter until tender.

9. Using **steel blade,** process green onions until finely chopped. Sauté in 4 tablespoons butter until tender.

10. Stir flour into green onions and cook about 3 minutes. Add wine, salt, and pepper. Gradually add milk, stirring constantly until thickened. Add mushrooms and nutmeg.

11. To assemble, remove roll from oven. Loosen edges from pan. Carefully lift roll and foil off of jelly-roll pan and remove to a large serving platter. Spread with half of the mushroom filling and carefully roll in a jelly-roll fashion, using foil as a pusher.

12. Remaining sauce can either be poured over the top or served separately on the side. Cut into slices and serve.

*10 to 12 servings*

# *Cheese-Spinach Gnocchi*

*Gnocchi:*
    ½ pound fresh spinach, cleaned and
        trimmed
    ½ small onion, peeled and cut in
        half
    2 tablespoons butter
    3 ounces Swiss cheese (1½ cups
        shredded)
    1½ cups milk
    ¼ teaspoon salt
        Pinch nutmeg
    ¼ cup uncooked farina
    1 egg

*Topping:*
    2 eggs
    1 tablespoon flour
    ¼ teaspoon salt
        Pinch nutmeg
    ¾ cup milk

1. For gnocchi, cook spinach until tender and drain thoroughly. Set aside.

2. Using **steel blade,** process onion until chopped. Sauté in 1 tablespoon butter until lightly browned.

3. Using **shredding disc,** shred cheese and set aside.

4. In a saucepan, bring milk, 1 tablespoon butter, salt, and nutmeg to boiling. Add farina gradually, stirring constantly over low heat until mixture thickens.

5. Using **steel blade,** add egg to bowl and beat lightly. Add farina mixture, spinach, onion, and 1 cup shredded cheese and process until thoroughly blended. Set aside to cool slightly.

6. Drop mixture by tablespoonfuls close together in a well-greased 9-inch shallow baking dish or casserole. Sprinkle mounds with remaining cheese.

7. For topping, using **steel blade,** add eggs to bowl and beat well. Add flour, salt, and nutmeg through feed tube with machine on, add milk through feed tube, and process until thoroughly mixed together. Pour mixture over spinach mounds.

8. Bake at 350°F about 35 to 40 minutes, or until puffy and golden brown.

*6 servings*

# Cold Cheese Mousse

½ small onion, peeled and cut in
   half
5 tablespoons butter
2 ounces Swiss cheese (1 cup
   shredded)
½ cup flour
1¼ cups milk, scalded
2 envelopes unflavored gelatin
½ cup chicken stock
4 eggs, separated
¼ teaspoon Dijon mustard
¼ teaspoon salt
   Pinch nutmeg
¼ cup whipping cream

   Rosy Mayonnaise

1. Using **steel blade,** process onion until finely chopped. In a saucepan, cook onion in 1 tablespoon butter until transparent.
2. Using **shredding disc,** shred cheese and set aside.
3. To cooked onion, add 4 tablespoons butter, stir in flour, and cook over a low heat, stirring constantly, for 3 minutes. Add milk and stir sauce with a whisk until thickened and smooth. Add shredded cheese and stir until cheese is melted. Remove from heat.
4. Soften gelatin in chicken stock. Stir over low heat until gelatin is dissolved.
5. Using **steel blade,** place cheese sauce in the bowl. With machine on, add gelatin mixture through the feed tube. Add egg yolks, mustard, salt, and nutmeg and process until creamy. Cool.
6. Meanwhile, using a mixer, beat egg whites until stiff, but not dry, peaks are formed. Also, using a mixer, whip the cream. Add stiffly beaten egg white and cheese mixture to whipped cream and gently fold together.
7. Turn mixture into a 2-quart mold rinsed with cold water. Chill for 3 hours, and unmold on a serving platter. Garnish with **watercress.** *Serve with Rosy Mayonnaise.*

*8 servings*

## Rosy Mayonnaise

1 egg
1 teaspoon Dijon mustard
½ teaspoon salt
1 tablespoon lemon juice
1 cup vegetable oil
1 teaspoon tomato paste or ketchup

1. Using **plastic blade,** put egg, Dijon mustard, and salt in the bowl and process for about 15 seconds, stopping to scrape down the bowl if necessary.
2. Add lemon juice and process a few seconds longer.
3. With machine on, add oil through the feed tube in a very slow, steady stream. Process until mayonnaise begins to thicken, at which point remaining oil can be added a bit faster. The longer the mayonnaise is processed, the thicker it will become.
4. When mayonnaise has reached desired consistency, add tomato paste and process until blended. More tomato paste or ketchup can be added for a stronger tomato flavor or a deeper shade.

*Note:* Mayonnaise will keep at least a week in a covered container in the refrigerator.

# VEGETABLES

# Asparagus Supreme

1 slice dry bread, cut in quarters
    (¼ cup crumbs)
2 ounces sharp Cheddar cheese
    (1 cup shredded)
1 small onion, peeled and quartered
2 tablespoons butter
1 tablespoon flour
¼ teaspoon salt
½ teaspoon paprika
¼ teaspoon dry mustard
½ teaspoon Worcestershire sauce
1 cup evaporated milk
2 pounds fresh asparagus, trimmed,
    cooked, and drained
1 tablespoon butter, melted

1. Using **steel blade,** process bread to fine crumbs. Set aside.
2. Using **shredding disc,** shred cheese and set aside.
3. Using **steel blade,** process onion until finely chopped. In a saucepan, cook onion in butter until tender, but not browned. Blend in flour, salt, paprika, dry mustard, and Worcestershire sauce. Heat until bubbly.
4. Remove from heat. Add evaporated milk gradually, stirring constantly. Return to heat; bring to boiling and cook 1 to 2 minutes.
5. Turn asparagus into a 1-quart shallow baking dish. Pour sauce over asparagus. Sprinkle with shredded cheese. Mix bread crumbs and melted butter together and sprinkle over the top.
6. Set under broiler with top of mixture 3 inches from heat and broil 3 to 5 minutes, or until crumbs are lightly browned and cheese is melted.

*6 to 8 servings*

# Broccoli, Sicilian Style

*tasty but cheese sauce congeals when reheated*

1 clove garlic
1 medium onion, peeled and cut to
    fit feed tube
2 tablespoons olive oil
1½ tablespoons flour
¼ teaspoon pepper
1 cup chicken stock *fresh only,*
3 ounces sharp Cheddar cheese (1½ *not frozen*
    cups shredded)
½ cup ripe olives
4 anchovy fillets
2 pounds fresh broccoli, cooked and
    drained

1. Using **steel blade,** mince garlic.
2. Using **slicing disc,** slice onion.
3. In a saucepan, cook onion and garlic in olive oil until onion is soft. Blend in a mixture of flour and pepper and heat until bubbly.
4. Add chicken stock, stirring constantly. Bring to boiling and cook 1 to 2 minutes, or until sauce thickens.
5. Using **shredding disc,** shred cheese.
6. Using **slicing disc,** slice olives.
7. Using **steel blade,** process anchovy fillets until finely chopped.
8. Add shredded cheese, sliced olives, and chopped anchovy fillets to sauce. Stir over low heat until cheese melts. Pour sauce over hot broccoli and serve immediately.

*6 servings*

# Bavarian Carrots

1 pound carrots, pared and cut in
  2½-inch pieces
1 tablespoon sugar
3 slices bacon
1 large onion, peeled and quartered
2 apples, pared, cored, and
  quartered
½ cup chicken stock
½ teaspoon salt
⅛ teaspoon pepper
  Pinch nutmeg

1. Place carrots horizontally in the feed tube and slice with **slicing disc.**
2. In a saucepan, cover carrots with water and add sugar; cook until barely tender. Drain thoroughly.
3. Meanwhile, in a large saucepan, cook bacon until crisp, reserving drippings. Drain well on paper towel. Using **steel blade,** process until coarsely chopped.
4. Still using **steel blade,** process onion until chopped. Sauté in bacon drippings until golden.
5. Slice apples with **slicing disc.** Add sliced apples and chopped bacon to onions and cook together for 5 minutes. Add cooked carrots and toss gently. Add chicken stock, salt, pepper, and nutmeg and simmer for 5 minutes.

*6 servings*

# Greek-Style Carrots and Green Beans

1 pound carrots, pared and cut in
  2½-inch pieces
1 clove garlic
1 medium onion, peeled and
  quartered
1 pound fresh green beans, cleaned,
  trimmed, and cut in 2½-inch
  pieces
2 tablespoons butter
2 tablespoons oil
1 can (15 ounces) tomato sauce
¼ teaspoon cinnamon
½ teaspoon salt
¼ teaspoon pepper

1. Place carrots horizontally in the feed tube and slice with **slicing disc.** Set aside.
2. Using **steel blade,** mince garlic. Add onion and process until chopped.
3. In a saucepan, sauté green beans, sliced carrots, onion, and garlic in butter and oil about 15 minutes.
4. Add tomato sauce, cinnamon, salt, and pepper; simmer, partially covered, until vegetables are tender (about 30 minutes).

*8 servings*

# Braised Cucumbers

¼ cup parsley, cleaned and trimmed
  (2 tablespoons chopped)
2 medium onions, peeled and
  quartered
4 tablespoons butter
6 large cucumbers
2 tablespoons flour
½ cup chicken stock
  Salt and pepper to taste
  Pinch sugar
2 tablespoons lemon juice
1 teaspoon dried dill
½ cup dairy sour cream
  Dash nutmeg

1. Using **steel blade,** separately process parsley and onions until chopped. Set aside.
2. In a saucepan, sauté chopped onion in butter until transparent.
3. Pare cucumbers, cut in half lengthwise, and remove seeds. Cut into 3-inch lengths.
4. Add cucumbers to sautéed onions and cook until lightly browned. Add flour and cook for 2 minutes. Add chicken stock, salt, pepper, sugar, and lemon juice. Sprinkle with chopped parsley and dill and simmer for 10 minutes. Just before serving, add sour cream and nutmeg. Bring to a boil and reduce heat. Simmer for 5 minutes.

*8 servings*

## Mushroom Kugel

5 matzoh
¼ cup fresh parsley, cleaned and trimmed (2 tablespoons chopped)
2 medium onions, peeled and quartered
¼ pound fresh mushrooms, cleaned and trimmed
2 tablespoons butter
1 egg
1 cup cottage cheese
½ teaspoon salt
¼ teaspoon pepper

1. Soak matzoh in cold water for 2 minutes. Squeeze out as much water as possible and set aside.
2. Using **steel blade,** separately process parsley and onions until chopped. Set aside.
3. Using **slicing disc,** slice mushrooms.
4. In a skillet, sauté chopped onion and sliced mushrooms in butter until onion is soft.
5. Using **plastic blade,** beat egg lightly. Add squeezed-out matzoh, mushroom-onion mixture, and remaining ingredients. Process, using quick on/off motions, until blended.
6. Pour into a buttered 2-quart casserole.
7. Bake at 375°F 40 to 45 minutes.

*6 servings*

## Hash Brown Potato Patties

1 ounce sharp Cheddar cheese (½ cup shredded)
2 tablespoons fresh parsley, cleaned and trimmed (1 tablespoon chopped)
½ small onion, peeled and cut in half
1 package (3 ounces) cream cheese, cut in half
2 tablespoons flour
½ teaspoon salt
½ teaspoon paprika
3 tablespoons evaporated milk
1 egg
3 medium potatoes, pared and cut to fit feed tube
Butter for frying

1. Using **shredding disc,** shred cheese and set aside.
2. Using **steel blade,** separately process parsley and onion until chopped. Set aside.
3. Using **steel blade,** add cream cheese to bowl and process until smooth. Add all ingredients except potatoes to bowl and process until thoroughly blended. Remove from bowl.
4. Using **shredding disc,** shred potatoes and remove from bowl.
5. Using **plastic blade,** add potatoes and cheese mixture to bowl and process, using quick on/off motions, until blended.
6. Heat butter in a heavy skillet over medium heat. Spoon about ¼ cup of mixture for each pancake into hot skillet and cook until golden brown and crisp on one side. Turn patties and brown other side. Drain on paper towels. Serve immediately.

*8 to 10 pancakes*

## Curried Scalloped Potatoes au Gratin

2 ounces sharp Cheddar cheese (1 cup shredded)
1 small onion, peeled and quartered
6 potatoes (long and narrow to fit feed tube), pared
3 tablespoons flour
1 teaspoon salt
⅛ teaspoon pepper
½ to 1 teaspoon curry powder
3 tablespoons butter
2½ cups milk, scalded

1. Using **shredding disc,** shred cheese and set aside.
2. Using **steel blade,** process onion until finely chopped and set aside.
3. Using **slicing disc,** slice potatoes.
4. Combine flour, salt, pepper, and curry powder and mix together.
5. In a well-greased 2-quart casserole, put a third of potato slices. Sprinkle with a third of the chopped onion and a third of flour mixture and half of the shredded cheese. Dot with 1 tablespoon of butter. Repeat layering twice, ending with butter. Pour scalded milk over the potatoes and cover.
6. Bake at 350°F 30 minutes. Remove cover and bake 60 to 70 minutes longer, or until potatoes are tender. Remove from oven and let stand about 5 minutes before serving.

*8 servings*

# Harvest Soufflé

3 **ounces sharp Cheddar cheese (1½ cups shredded)**
4 **tablespoons butter**
¼ **cup flour**
¼ **teaspoon salt**
⅛ **teaspoon garlic powder**
⅓ **cup milk**
1 **can (17 ounces) cream-style corn**
½ **teaspoon Worcestershire sauce**
6 **eggs, separated**

1. Using **shredding disc,** shred cheese and set aside.
2. In a saucepan, melt butter, add flour, salt, and garlic powder and heat until bubbly. Remove from heat and blend in milk, corn, and Worcestershire sauce. Return to heat and bring mixture to a boil, stirring constantly. Cook 2 minutes and remove from heat.
3. Add shredded cheese and stir until cheese is melted.
4. Using **plastic blade,** add egg yolks to bowl and process until well beaten. Add corn mixture and process until thoroughly blended, stopping to scrape down sides, if necessary.
5. Using a mixer, beat egg whites until stiff, not dry, peaks are formed. Gently spread egg-yolk mixture over egg whites. Carefully fold together until just blended. Gently turn the mixture into an ungreased 2-quart soufflé dish (deep casserole with straight sides).
6. Bake at 350°F 40 to 45 minutes, or until a knife inserted in the center of the soufflé comes out clean. Serve immediately.

*6 servings*

# Scalloped Corn Fiesta

12 **ritz crackers**
1 **ounce sharp Cheddar cheese (½ cup shredded)**
1 **medium carrot, pared and cut in 1-inch pieces**
½ **medium green pepper, trimmed and cut in 1-inch pieces**
1 **stalk celery, trimmed and cut in 1-inch pieces**
½ **small onion, peeled and halved**
2 **eggs**
1 **can (17 ounces) cream-style corn**
½ **teaspoon sugar**
½ **teaspoon salt**
6 **drops Tabasco**
4 **tablespoons butter, melted**
¼ **cup evaporated milk**

1. Using **steel blade,** process crackers to fine crumbs and set aside.
2. Using **shredding disc,** shred cheese and set aside.
3. Using **steel blade,** separately process carrot until finely chopped, green pepper until coarsely chopped, celery until coarsely chopped, and onion until finely chopped. Remove each from bowl and set aside.
4. Using **plastic blade,** add eggs to bowl and beat lightly. Add all ingredients to bowl, except shredded cheese, and process until thoroughly blended.
5. Turn into a greased 8×8×2-inch baking dish and top with cheese. Sprinkle with paprika, if desired.
6. Bake at 350°F 30 minutes, or until custard is set and top is golden brown.

*6 servings*

# Baked Herb Potato Pancake

¼ cup fresh parsley, cleaned and trimmed (2 tablespoons chopped)
1 medium onion, peeled and quartered
3 eggs
½ cup flour
8 tablespoons butter, melted
1 teaspoon tarragon
1 teaspoon chervil
Pinch nutmeg
1 teaspoon salt
¼ teaspoon pepper
3 pounds large potatoes, pared and cut to fit feed tube

1. Using **steel blade,** separately process parsley and onion until chopped and set aside.
2. Using **plastic blade,** add eggs to bowl and process until frothy. Add flour, 4 tablespoons melted butter, tarragon, chervil, nutmeg, salt, pepper, and chopped parsley. Process until well blended and remove from bowl.
3. Using **shredding disc,** shred potatoes and remove from bowl.
4. Using **plastic blade,** add half shredded potatoes and half egg mixture to bowl and process, using quick on/off motions, until blended. Repeat, using remaining ingredients.
5. Heavily butter two 9-inch round cake pans. Spread potato mixture evenly in pans. Pour remaining melted butter over the tops.
6. Bake at 375°F about 45 minutes, or until edges are golden. Remove from pan and cut into wedges.

*8 servings*

# Rutabaga au Gratin

1 rutabaga (1½ pounds), pared and cut to fit feed tube
2 slices dry bread, cut in quarters (½ cup crumbs)
2 ounces sharp Cheddar cheese (1 cup shredded)
6 tablespoons butter
¼ cup flour
2 cups hot milk
¼ teaspoon salt
Dash pepper
Pinch nutmeg

1. Using **slicing disc,** slice rutabaga. In a saucepan, cover with salted water and cook, covered, until tender. Drain thoroughly. You should have 4 cups cooked sliced rutabaga.
2. Using **steel blade,** process bread to fine crumbs and set aside.
3. Using **shredding disc,** shred cheese and set aside.
4. In a saucepan, melt 4 tablespoons butter, stir in flour and cook 1 to 2 minutes. Add hot milk and stir with a whisk until thickened and smooth. Add shredded cheese and stir until melted. Add salt, pepper, and nutmeg.
5. Put cooked rutabaga in a 1½-quart casserole. Pour cheese sauce over top.
6. Melt remaining 2 tablespoons of butter and mix with bread crumbs. Sprinkle mixture over the top of casserole.
7. Bake at 400°F about 15 minutes.

*6 servings*

# Mushrooms Magnifique

1 slice dry bread, cut in quarters (¼ cup crumbs)
1 small clove garlic
¼ cup fresh parsley, cleaned and trimmed (2 tablespoons chopped)
½ cup pecans
12 large fresh mushrooms, cleaned
2 tablespoons butter, melted
¼ teaspoon salt
⅛ teaspoon thyme
½ cup whipping cream

1. Using **steel blade,** separately process bread to fine crumbs, garlic until minced, parsley and pecans until chopped. Set aside.
2. Remove stems from mushrooms. Using **steel blade,** process enough stems to make ½ cup finely chopped mushrooms. Remove from bowl.
3. Using **plastic blade,** add all ingredients except cream to bowl and process until blended.
4. Heap mixture into mushroom caps and place in a shallow baking dish. Pour cream over all.
5. Bake at 350°F about 20 minutes, or until mushrooms are tender, basting several times with the cream.

*12 stuffed mushrooms*

# Rutabaga Soufflé

1 slice dry bread (¼ cup crumbs)
1 cube (1 inch) Parmesan cheese
    (2 tablespoons grated)
1 small rutabaga, pared and cut to
    fit feed tube
1 cup milk
2 tablespoons cornstarch
½ teaspoon salt
⅛ teaspoon pepper
1 tablespoon brown sugar
¼ teaspoon ground mace
3 eggs, separated
1 tablespoon butter, melted

1. Using **steel blade,** separately process bread into fine crumbs and cheese to a fine powder and set aside.
2. Using **slicing disc,** slice rutabaga. In a saucepan, cover with salted water and cook, covered, until tender. Drain thoroughly.
3. Using **steel blade,** process cooked rutabaga until puréed and remove from bowl. You should have 2 cups purée.
4. Blend milk with cornstarch in a saucepan. Bring to boiling over low heat; stir and cook about 3 minutes. Stir in salt, pepper, brown sugar, and mace.
5. Using **plastic blade,** add egg yolks to bowl and beat lightly. With machine running, add hot mixture gradually through feed tube. Add rutabaga purée and process until thoroughly blended.
6. Using a mixer, beat egg whites until stiff, not dry, peaks are formed. Gently spread rutabaga mixture over egg whites. Gently fold together until just blended. Turn into a 1½-quart casserole.
7. Toss bread crumbs with butter and grated Parmesan cheese and spoon over top of soufflé.
8. Bake at 325°F about 50 minutes, or until a knife comes out clean when inserted in center of the soufflé. Serve at once.

*6 servings*

# Spinach Pie

*Pie Crust:*
  1½ cups flour
    6 tablespoons butter, frozen and cut
      in pieces
  2½ tablespoons vegetable shortening
    ½ teaspoon salt
  4½ tablespoons ice water

*Filling:*
  1½ pounds fresh spinach or 2
      packages (10 ounces each)
      frozen spinach
    6 ounces sharp Cheddar or Swiss
      cheese (3 cups shredded)
    1 clove garlic
    1 medium onion, peeled and
      quartered
    5 tablespoons butter
    3 tablespoons flour
  1½ cups milk
    1 teaspoon salt
    ¼ teaspoon pepper
    Pinch nutmeg
    6 eggs

1. For crust, using **steel blade,** combine flour, butter, shortening, and salt in bowl and process until cut together.
2. With machine on, add water through feed tube and process until mixture forms into a ball.
3. Roll out dough, line a 10-inch pie plate, and flute pastry edge.
4. For filling, wash fresh spinach and cook, using only water left on leaves, until tender. Squeeze out as much water as possible. Using **steel blade,** process spinach until finely chopped and set aside.
5. Using **shredding disc,** shred cheese and set aside.
6. Using **steel blade,** mince garlic. Add onion and process until finely chopped.
7. In a skillet, heat 2 tablespoons butter and sauté onion and garlic until golden. Stir in spinach.
8. In a saucepan, melt 3 tablespoons butter, add flour, and cook 1 to 2 minutes. Gradually add milk, stirring with a whisk until thickened and smooth. Add salt, pepper, nutmeg, and spinach mixture.
9. Using **plastic blade,** add eggs to bowl and beat until frothy. Add spinach and 2 cups cheese and process until thoroughly blended. Pour mixture into pie shell.
10. Bake at 350°F 30 minutes. Add remaining shredded cheese on top and bake 10 to 15 minutes longer, or until puffed and firm to the touch in the center.

*10 to 12 servings*

# Sweet Potato Tzimmes

1 pound sweet potatoes, pared and
   cut to fit feed tube
1 can (16 ounces) grapefruit sections
12 prunes, cooked and pitted
2 tablespoons honey
2 tablespoons brown sugar
¼ teaspoon nutmeg
½ teaspoon salt
3 tablespoons butter

1. Using **slicing disc,** slice sweet potatoes. Cook until almost tender (about 10 to 15 minutes) and drain.
2. Drain grapefruit sections, reserving liquid.
3. Arrange alternating layers of cooked sweet potatoes, grapefruit sections, and prunes in a 1½-quart casserole.
4. Measure ¼ cup grapefruit liquid and combine it with honey, brown sugar, nutmeg, and salt. Pour mixture over casserole and dot with butter.
5. Bake at 375°F about 30 minutes.

*6 servings*

# Baked Stuffed Sweet Potatoes

4 medium sweet potatoes
¼ cup pecans
1 ripe banana, cut in 1-inch pieces
2 tablespoons butter, softened
⅓ cup orange juice
1 tablespoon brown sugar
½ teaspoon salt
⅛ teaspoon nutmeg

1. Bake sweet potatoes at 375°F 45 to 60 minutes, or until tender when tested with a fork.
2. Using **steel blade,** process pecans until coarsely chopped and set aside.
3. Using **steel blade,** add banana, butter, orange juice, brown sugar, salt, and nutmeg to bowl and process until smooth.
4. Cut a lengthwise slice off the top of each sweet potato and scoop out center. Reserve shells. Add potato to bowl and process, using quick on/off motions, until blended.
5. Spoon mixture into shells. Sprinkle with chopped pecans. Set on a cookie sheet.
6. Return to oven 12 to 15 minutes, or until heated.

*4 servings*

# Stuffed Zucchini

4 slices dry bread, cut in quarters
   (1 cup crumbs)
4 cubes (1 inch each) Parmesan
   cheese (½ cup grated)
½ cup fresh parsley, cleaned and
   trimmed (¼ cup chopped)
2 cloves garlic
4 large or 8 small zucchini
4 tablespoons butter
¾ pound bulk pork sausage (or
   Italian sausage)
2 eggs
1 teaspoon rosemary
¼ cup whipping cream
½ teaspoon salt
¼ teaspoon pepper

1. Using **steel blade,** separately process bread to fine crumbs, Parmesan cheese to a fine powder, parsley until chopped, and garlic until minced.
2. Trim end of zucchini. Split zucchini in half lengthwise and scoop out pulp, leaving shell for stuffing. Sauté zucchini pulp in butter until tender.
3. Meanwhile, cook sausage. Pour off fat and drain well.
4. Using **plastic blade,** lightly beat 2 eggs; add cooked sausage, zucchini pulp, minced garlic, rosemary, cream, chopped parsley, bread crumbs, salt, pepper, and half of Parmesan cheese. Using quick on/off motions, process to thoroughly mix ingredients.
5. Fill zucchini halves with mixture and sprinkle with remaining cheese.
6. Butter a large shallow baking pan. Place stuffed zucchini in pan.
7. Bake at 350°F 30 minutes, or until zucchini is tender and stuffing is golden.

*8 servings*

# Zucchini-Tomato Pie

**Pie Crust:**
- 1 cup flour
- 4 tablespoons butter, frozen and cut in pieces
- 1½ tablespoons vegetable shortening
- ¼ teaspoon salt
- 3 tablespoons ice water

**Filling:**
- 4 cubes (1 inch each) Parmesan cheese (½ cup grated)
- ½ cup fresh parsley, cleaned and trimmed (¼ cup chopped)
- 1 clove garlic
- 2 medium onions, peeled and quartered
- 3 tablespoons vegetable oil
- 2 small zucchini, cut in 3½-inch pieces
- 4 large tomatoes
- ¾ teaspoon salt
- ¼ teaspoon pepper
- 2 eggs
- ¼ cup whipping cream

1. For crust, using **steel blade,** combine flour, butter, shortening, and salt in bowl and process until cut together.
2. With machine on, add ice water through feed tube and process until mixture forms into a ball.
3. Roll out dough, line a 9-inch pie plate, and flute pastry edge. Prick the bottom with a fork. Line with foil or parchment paper, and fill with dried beans or rice.
4. Bake at 450°F 8 minutes. Remove foil and beans and cook 4 minutes longer.
5. For filling, using **steel blade,** separately process Parmesan cheese to a fine powder, parsley until chopped, garlic until minced, and onions until finely chopped. Remove each from bowl.
6. In a skillet, sauté onion and garlic in oil until browned.
7. Using **slicing disc,** slice zucchini. Slice tomatoes by hand. Add sliced zucchini and tomatoes to skillet and sauté until tender.
8. Pour the vegetable mixture into partially baked pie shell. through the feed tube. Pour the mixture over the vegetables and top with grated Parmesan cheese.
10. Bake at 400°F 15 to 20 minutes, or until custard is set and pastry is golden.

*8 servings*

# Rice Pilaf

- 2 cups uncooked rice
- 8 tablespoons butter
- ½ cup fresh parsley, cleaned and trimmed (¼ cup chopped)
- 5 cups chicken stock

1. In a saucepan, brown rice in butter until golden.
2. Using **steel blade,** process parsley until chopped.
3. Add chicken stock and chopped parsley to rice. Cover and bring to a boil. Reduce heat and gently simmer 20 to 30 minutes, or until liquid is absorbed and rice is tender.

*8 servings*

# Spanish Rice au Gratin

- 2 ounces sharp Cheddar cheese (1 cup shredded)
- ½ cup uncooked rice
- 1 cup chicken stock
- 2 stalks celery, cut in 1-inch pieces
- 1 medium onion, peeled and quartered
- 1 small green pepper, cut in 1-inch pieces
- 2 tablespoons butter
- 2 medium tomatoes or 1 can (18 ounces) whole tomatoes
- 1 teaspoon sugar
- ¾ teaspoon chili powder
- ¼ teaspoon Worcestershire sauce
- Salt and pepper

1. Using **shredding disc,** shred cheese. Remove from bowl and set aside.
2. Combine rice and chicken stock in a saucepan. Bring to boiling, reduce heat, and simmer, covered, about 15 minutes.
3. Meanwhile, using **steel blade,** separately process celery, onion, and green pepper until chopped.
4. Heat butter in a skillet and sauté chopped vegetables until tender. Add cooked rice, tomatoes cut in pieces, sugar, chili powder, and Worcestershire sauce. Simmer until thick. Season with salt and pepper to taste.
5. Turn rice mixture into a greased baking dish. Top evenly with shredded cheese.
6. Place under a broiler 3 to 4 inches from the heat until cheese is melted. Serve immediately.

*4 servings*

# Ratatouille Provençal

½ cup fresh parsley, cleaned and trimmed (¼ cup chopped)
2 cloves garlic
2 small onions, peeled
1 medium green pepper, trimmed and cored
  Olive oil (9 tablespoons or more)
2 small zucchini, cut in 3½-inch pieces
½ medium eggplant (about ½ pound), pared and cut in lengthwise halves
5 medium tomatoes, or 1 can (28 ounces) whole tomatoes, drained
1 teaspoon salt
½ teaspoon pepper

1. Using **steel blade,** separately process parsley until chopped and garlic until minced.
2. Using **slicing disc,** slice onions and pepper. In a skillet or Dutch oven, sauté sliced onion and pepper in 3 tablespoons olive oil until tender but not browned. Remove from skillet.
3. Using **slicing disc,** slice zucchini and sauté in 3 tablespoons or more of olive oil until lightly browned. (Be careful to handle all vegetables delicately with a wooden spoon. Slices should remain whole.) Remove from skillet.
4. Using **slicing disc,** slice eggplant and sauté in 3 tablespoons or more of olive oil until lightly browned. Remove from skillet.
5. Cut fresh tomatoes or canned, drained tomatoes in thick slices.
6. In a large saucepan, arrange a third of tomatoes on bottom. Add half of onion and pepper mixture, then half of eggplant, then half of zucchini. Sprinkle with salt, pepper, and chopped parsley. Add another third of tomatoes, then remainder of onion-pepper mixture, eggplant, and zucchini. Top with remaining tomatoes, parsley, salt, and pepper.
7. Cover and simmer for 10 minutes. Remove the cover and simmer about 15 minutes longer.

*4 servings*

*Note:* Ratatouille is an excellent side dish for roast meats or sautéed chicken. It is best when made a day in advance to allow flavors to blend. It can be served either hot or cold and is an excellent summer picnic dish.

# Pork Fried Rice

1 medium onion, peeled and quartered
1 cup cooked roast pork, cut in 1-inch pieces
½ cup cooked shrimp
3 to 4 green onions
½ cup fresh bean sprouts
½ cup green peas
4 cups cold cooked rice
2 tablespoons soy sauce
1 tablespoon sherry
½ teaspoon salt

1. Using **steel blade,** separately process onion until chopped, roast pork and cooked shrimp until coarsely chopped. Remove each from bowl and set aside.
2. Using **slicing disc,** slice green onions.
3. Blanch bean sprouts by pouring boiling water over them. Stir for a couple of seconds, then drain in a colander. Rinse immediately with cold water and drain again.
4. Parboil green peas by adding to boiling water; cook for a couple of minutes until they turn bright green. Drain in a colander, rinse immediately with cold water, and drain again.
5. Heat 2 tablespoons oil in a wok or skillet. Stir-fry chopped onions until transparent. Add chopped pork, chopped shrimp, sliced scallion, blanched bean sprouts, and parboiled peas and stir-fry to coat with oil.
6. Break up the cold cooked rice so that rice is not lumpy. Add rice, soy sauce, sherry, and salt and stir-fry to heat thoroughly. If necessary, a few additional drops of oil can be added. Also, 2 eggs, slightly scrambled, can be added.
7. Serve hot.

*6 servings*

**From the Russian dinner menu on page 8:**
**Braised Cucumbers, 57, and Russian Salmon**
**Mound, 44**

# SALADS

From the Italian dinner menu on page 8: Italian
Bread, 74, Chocolate-Ricotta Cheese Cake, 85,
and Cheese Ravioli with Tomato Sauce, 38

# Green Salad Vinaigrette

1 hard-cooked egg
1 clove garlic
2 tablespoons fresh parsley, cleaned and trimmed (1 tablespoon chopped)
⅛ teaspoon chervil
⅛ teaspoon tarragon
1 teaspoon Dijon mustard
1 tablespoon wine vinegar
1 tablespoon lemon juice
4 tablespoons vegetable oil
.2 tablespoons olive oil
¼ teaspoon salt
⅛ teaspoon pepper
1 head romaine lettuce

1. Using **plastic blade,** process hard-cooked egg until finely chopped. Set aside.
2. Using **steel blade,** mince garlic. Add parsley and process until chopped. Add remaining ingredients, except chopped hard-cooked egg and romaine, and process until thoroughly blended.
3. Wash and thoroughly dry romaine; tear into pieces into a salad bowl, pour dressing over lettuce, and gently toss together. Sprinkle chopped hard-cooked egg over the top.

*8 servings*

# Spinach Salad with Hot Sweet and Sour Dressing

½ pound bacon
1 medium onion, peeled and quartered
1 pound fresh spinach

**Dressing:**
¼ cup water
¼ cup vinegar
½ cup sugar
1½ cups mayonnaise

1. Cook bacon until crisp and set aside. Reserve 1 tablespoon bacon drippings.
2. Using **steel blade,** process onion until chopped and cook in bacon drippings until golden.
3. Wash and trim spinach and drain thoroughly.
4. For dressing, combine water, vinegar, and sugar in a saucepan and boil until sugar dissolves. Add mayonnaise and onion and heat thoroughly, stirring until smooth.
5. Using **steel blade,** process bacon, using quick on/off motions, until coarsely chopped.
6. Pour hot salad dressing over spinach, sprinkle bacon over top, and toss gently.

*6 to 8 servings*

*Note:* Any leftover salad dressing can be stored in refrigerator and reheated before serving.

# Greek Salad

**Salad Dressing:**
- ⅓ cup olive oil
- ¼ cup wine vinegar
- ½ teaspoon salt
- 1 teaspoon oregano

**Salad:**
- 1 large head romaine, trimmed and torn in pieces
- 1 cucumber, pared and cut in 3½-inch pieces
- 1 small bunch radishes, cleaned and trimmed
- 2 small green peppers, trimmed and cored
- 1 can (8 ounces) whole beets, drained
- 4 tomatoes
- ⅓ pound feta cheese
  Greek olives
  Anchovy fillets (optional)

1. For salad dressing, mix all ingredients and refrigerate.
2. For salad, put romaine pieces in a large salad bowl.
3. Using **slicing disc,** slice cucumber, radishes, green pepper, and beets.
4. Cut tomatoes into quarters.
5. Using **plastic blade,** process feta cheese, using quick on/off motions, until crumbled.
6. Combine prepared salad ingredients with romaine in a bowl, sprinkle with crumbled feta cheese, and top with olives and, if desired, anchovy fillets. Pour salad dressing over salad and serve.

*8 servings*

# Pimento Cheese-Avocado Salad

**Salad:**
- 4 ripe avocados
  Lemon juice
- 1 jar (7 ounces) whole pimentos, drained
- ⅓ cup fresh parsley, cleaned and trimmed (3 tablespoons chopped)
- 1 package (8 ounces) cream cheese, cut in quarters
- 1 tablespoon capers
  Pinch cayenne pepper
- ½ teaspoon salt
- ⅛ teaspoon pepper
  Salad greens

**Dressing:**
- 1 whole pimento, drained
- ½ cup mayonnaise
- ½ cup dairy sour cream
- ¼ teaspoon salt
- ⅛ teaspoon pepper
- 2 tablespoons lemon juice

1. For salad, cut avocados into halves, peel, and remove pits. Enlarge the pit cavities with a spoon, reserving scooped-out avocado. Score the surfaces of cavities with a fork. Brush surface (except cavities) with lemon juice.
2. Pat pimentos dry with a paper towel. Keep pimentos in one piece. Line the avocado cavities with the pimentos and trim evenly around the edges. Set leftover pimento aside.
3. Using **steel blade,** process parsley until chopped. Set aside.
4. Using **plastic blade,** process cream cheese until smooth. Add 2 tablespoons chopped parsley, scooped-out avocado, leftover pimento, capers, cayenne pepper, salt, and pepper. Process until thoroughly blended.
5. Fill the lined avocado with the cheese mixture, spreading it smoothly on the top. Cover and chill thoroughly.
6. For dressing, using **plastic blade,** add all ingredients to the bowl and process until thoroughly blended. Chill thoroughly.
7. When ready to serve, halve each filled avocado shell lengthwise and arrange quarters on crisp salad greens. Serve with dressing on the side.

*8 servings*

# Piquant Pepper-Cabbage Slaw

¼ to ⅓ cup sugar
2 tablespoons flour
½ teaspoon salt
2 teaspoons dry mustard
2 eggs, fork beaten
1 cup milk, scalded
¾ cup cider vinegar
2 tablespoons butter
1 teaspoon celery seed
1 medium head cabbage, trimmed
  and cut in wedges to fit feed tube
1 green pepper, trimmed and cut in
  1-inch pieces
1 red pepper, trimmed and cut in
  1-inch pieces

1. In the top of a double boiler, mix sugar, flour, salt, and dry mustard. Blend in eggs and milk. Cook over boiling water about 5 minutes, stirring frequently.
2. Stir in vinegar, a small amount at a time. Cook and stir until mixture begins to thicken, then mix in the butter and celery seed. Remove from heat. Cool and chill thoroughly.
3. Using **shredding disc** or **slicing disc,** shred or slice cabbage, depending on desired consistency.
4. Using **steel blade,** process peppers one at a time, until finely chopped.
5. To serve, toss cabbage and peppers with enough dressing to coat evenly. (Store the remaining dressing.) Mound into fresh spinach leaves, if desired.

*8 servings*

# Fresh Corn Vinaigrette

¼ cup fresh parsley, cleaned and
  trimmed (2 tablespoons finely
  chopped)
½ medium green pepper, trimmed
  and cut in 1-inch pieces
2 green onions, trimmed and cut in
  1-inch pieces
¼ cup vegetable oil
2 tablespoons wine vinegar
1 teaspoon lemon juice
1 teaspoon salt
½ teaspoon sugar
¼ teaspoon basil
⅛ teaspoon ground red pepper
1 large tomato
1 can (12 ounces) whole kernel corn,
  drained

1. Using **steel blade,** separately process parsley, green pepper, and green onions until finely chopped and remove from bowl.
2. Using **plastic blade,** add oil, vinegar, lemon juice, salt, sugar, basil, and red pepper to the bowl and process until thoroughly blended. Add parsley, green pepper, and green onion and process for a second or two until combined.
3. Chop tomato by hand.
4. In a large bowl, combine drained corn and chopped tomato. Add dressing and toss to mix well.
5. Cover and chill for several hours.
6. Serve as a relish or with **salad greens.**

*4 to 6 servings*

# Fruit Salad Medley

3 oranges, peeled and separated in
  half
1 apple, pared, cored, and quartered
1 pear, pared, cored, and halved
2 bananas, peeled and cut in 3½-inch
  pieces
¼ cup sugar
1 package (10 ounces) frozen
  raspberries or strawberries,
  thawed and drained (or ½ pound
  fresh)
3 tablespoons curacao or kirsch

1. Cut a thin slice off bottom and top of orange halves, apple quarters, pear quarters, and banana pieces, so that they sit flat on blade in the feed tube. Slice each fruit with **slicing disc** and remove to a decorative crystal bowl as they are sliced. Toss gently so that apple, pear, and banana slices are coated with orange juice to prevent them from discoloring.
2. Add sugar and toss again. Refrigerate for 2 hours.
3. About ½ hour before serving, add raspberries or strawberries and liqueur and toss gently. Garnish with **fresh mint,** if available.

*6 servings*

# Blue Cheese Potato Salad

5 medium potatoes, pared, cooked,
    and diced
½ teaspoon salt
¼ teaspoon pepper
4 hard-cooked eggs
3 stalks celery, trimmed and cut in
    1-inch pieces
4 green onions, trimmed and cut in
    1-inch pieces
½ medium green pepper, trimmed
    and cut in 1-inch pieces
1 cup cottage cheese
½ teaspoon dry mustard
¼ teaspoon salt
⅛ teaspoon pepper
⅔ cup (6-ounce can) evaporated milk
½ cup crumbled blue cheese
2 tablespoons cider vinegar
    Lettuce
    Green pepper slices and tomato
    wedges for garnish

1. Put potatoes into a large bowl and sprinkle with salt and pepper.
2. Using **steel blade,** process hard-cooked eggs, using quick on/off motions, until finely chopped. Add to potatoes.
3. Using **steel blade,** separately process celery, green onion, and green pepper until finely chopped. Add to potatoes and toss lightly.
4. Using **steel blade,** put cottage cheese, dry mustard, salt, pepper, evaporated milk, blue cheese, and vinegar in the bowl. Process until thoroughly blended.
5. Pour dressing over potato mixture in bowl and toss lightly and thoroughly. Chill well before serving to blend the flavors.
2. Spoon chilled potato salad into a bowl lined with lettuce. Garnish with green pepper slices and tomato wedges.

*8 servings*

# Mexican Christmas Eve Salad

*Salad:*
4 ounces peanuts (¾ cup)
1 head lettuce, cut in wedges
2 oranges, peeled and halved
2 bananas, peeled and cut in
    3½-inch lengths
2 apples, pared, cored, and
    quartered
1 can (8 ounces) sliced pineapple
1 can (8 ounces) whole beets
    Juice of 1 lime

*Dressing:*
2 tablespoons white wine vinegar
1½ teaspoons sugar
¼ teaspoon salt
⅓ cup salad oil

1. For salad, using **steel blade,** process peanuts, with quick on/off motions, until coarsely chopped. Set aside.
2. Using **slicing disc,** slice lettuce and place in a large salad bowl.
3. Using **slicing disc,** slice oranges, bananas, and apples and remove to a large bowl.
4. Using **steel blade,** separately process pineapple and beets until coarsely chopped and remove to bowl with sliced fruit.
5. Mix beet-fruit mixture with lime juice.
6. For dressing, using **plastic blade,** combine all ingredients in bowl and process until thoroughly blended. Add desired amount of dressing to fruit and gently toss until evenly mixed and coated with dressing.
7. Mound fruit on top of sliced lettuce and sprinkle with chopped peanuts.

*8 to 10 servings*

# Cucumber Salmon Ring

1 package (3 ounces) lime-flavored
   gelatin
¼ teaspoon salt
1 cup boiling water
1 cup cold water
3 tablespoons lemon juice
1 large or 2 medium cucumbers
1 envelope unflavored gelatin
¼ cup cold water
½ teaspoon salt
2 tablespoons cider vinegar
2 stalks celery
4 ounces sweet pickles (about ¾ cup)
1 can (16 ounces) salmon, drained
   and flaked

1. Dissolve lime gelatin with ¼ teaspoon salt in boiling water. Stir in cold water and lemon juice. Chill until slightly thicker than thick, unbeaten egg white.
2. Pare cucumber and cut in half lengthwise. Scoop out seeds and dry cucumber on paper towel. Cut in 3½-inch pieces and shred with **shredding disc.** Stir shredded cucumber into slightly thickened lime gelatin. Turn into a 1½-quart ring mold. Chill until set, but not firm.
3. Meanwhile, soften unflavored gelatin in ¼ cup cold water. Set over low heat and stir until gelatin is dissolved. Blend with a mixture of mayonnaise, salt, and vinegar.
4. Using **steel blade,** separately process celery and sweet pickles until coarsely chopped. Remove from bowl.
5. Using **plastic blade,** add salmon, chopped celery and sweet pickle, and mayonnaise mixture to bowl and process until thoroughly blended.
6. Spoon salmon mixture into mold over first layer, which is just set, but not firm. Chill until firm.
7. Unmold on a serving plate and garnish with **salad greens.**

*8 servings*

# Ham Mousse with Spicy Gelatin Cubes

**Mousse:**
2 envelopes unflavored gelatin
1 cup cold water
2 tablespoons prepared mustard
   Pinch cayenne pepper
1 pound cooked ham, cut in 1-inch
   cubes
4 ounces pimento
6 small sweet pickles, cut in 1-inch
   pieces
1 cup whipping cream

**Gelatin Cubes:**
1½ cups peach syrup, drained from
   peach halves
½ cup thawed orange juice
   concentrate
2 tablespoons brown sugar
6 tablespoons lemon juice
2 tablespoons soy sauce
1 tablespoon minced onion
   Dash salt
⅛ teaspoon cloves
⅛ teaspoon allspice
1 package (3 ounces)
   cherry-flavored gelatin
⅓ cup water
¼ teaspoon almond extract

1. For mousse, in a saucepan, soften gelatin in cold water. Dissolve completely over low heat.
2. Remove from heat. Stir in mustard and cayenne pepper and cool. Chill until mixture is slightly thickened.
3. Using **steel blade,** process ham, a half pound at a time, until finely chopped. Remove from bowl and set aside.
4. Also using **steel blade,** separately process pimento and sweet pickle until coarsely chopped.
5. Using **plastic blade,** return chopped ingredients to the bowl. Add slightly thickened gelatin mixture and process until thoroughly blended, stopping to scrape down ingredients.
6. Using a mixer, beat cream. Add ham mixture to cream and gently fold together.
7. Turn mixture into a 1½-quart mold and chill until firm.

8. For gelatin cubes, combine in a saucepan the peach syrup, orange juice concentrate, brown sugar, lemon juice, soy sauce, minced onion, salt, cloves, and allspice. Bring to boiling, stirring until sugar is dissolved. Cover and simmer 10 minutes.
9. Pour peach liquid over gelatin and stir until gelatin is dissolved. Stir in water and almond extract. Pour into an 8-inch square pan and chill until firm.
10. When ready to serve, cut gelatin into 1-inch cubes. Unmold mousse onto a chilled serving plate. Garnish top of mold with pimento strips and spoon gelatin cubes around mold.

*8 servings*

# Dubonnet Chicken Salad Mold

3 envelopes unflavored gelatin
1 cup cranberry juice cocktail
1 cup red Dubonnet
1 cup red currant syrup
¾ cup cold water
1 tablespoon soy sauce
1 cup mayonnaise
¼ cup almonds
1 pound boneless chicken breasts,
    cooked and cut in 1-inch cubes
2 stalks celery, trimmed and cut in
    2-inch pieces
½ cup whipping cream

1. In a saucepan, sprinkle 2 envelopes gelatin over the cranberry juice to soften. Stir over low heat until gelatin is dissolved. Remove from heat and stir in the Dubonnet and syrup.
2. Pour into a 2-quart fancy tubed mold. Chill until almost set, but not firm.
3. Meanwhile, in a saucepan, sprinkle 1 envelope gelatin over cold water. Stir over low heat until gelatin is dissolved.
4. Remove from heat and stir in the soy sauce and mayonnaise until thoroughly blended. Chill until mixture is slightly thickened.
5. Using **steel blade,** separately process almonds, chicken, and celery until finely chopped.
6. When mayonnaise mixture is slightly thickened, add it to bowl with **plastic blade.** Add chopped chicken, celery, and almonds and process until thoroughly blended.
7. Using a mixer, whip cream and fold together with the chicken mixture.
8. Spoon mixture into mold over the first layer, which should be almost set, but not firm. Chill until firm (8 hours or overnight).
9. Unmold and garnish with **leaf lettuce, scored cucumber slices,** and **radish roses.**

*8 to 10 servings*

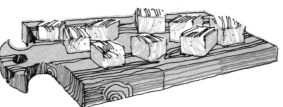

# Cucumber Mousse

3 large cucumbers
2 envelopes unflavored gelatin
2 green onions, green part only
1 package (8 ounces) cream cheese,
    cut in quarters
2 cups cottage cheese
1 teaspoon salt
    Dash pepper
1 teaspoon lemon juice
¼ teaspoon curry powder
    Parsley sprigs, cucumber slices,
    and lemon slices for garnish

1. Pare cucumbers. Cut in halves lengthwise and scoop out seeds. Cut into 2-inch pieces.
2. Using **steel blade,** process cucumber until finely chopped. Put into a strainer and let stand to drain thoroughly, reserving liquid.
3. Add enough water to cucumber liquid to make 1 cup and pour into a saucepan. Sprinkle gelatin over cucumber liquid and stir over low heat until gelatin is dissolved.
4. Using **steel blade,** process green onions until coarsely chopped. Add cream cheese, cottage cheese, salt, pepper, lemon juice, curry powder, and chopped cucumbers and process until smooth and creamy. With machine on, add gelatin mixture through the feed tube and process until blended.
5. Pour mixture into a 1-quart mold. Chill until firm. Unmold by dipping mold into lukewarm water for a few seconds. Garnish with parsley, cucumber slices, and lemon slices.

*6 servings*

# Avocado Mousse

1 envelope unflavored gelatin
1 cup water
4 medium, ripe avocados, peeled,
   pitted, and cut in pieces
½ cup mayonnaise
3 tablespoons lemon juice
¾ teaspoon salt
1 teaspoon prepared horseradish
½ cup whipping cream
   Watercress for garnish

1. In a saucepan, sprinkle gelatin over ½ cup of the water. Stir over low heat until gelatin is dissolved. Remove from heat and stir in remaining ½ cup water. Set gelatin aside to cool.

2. Meanwhile, using **steel blade,** add avocado and remaining ingredients, except cream, to the bowl. Process until smooth and creamy.

3. With machine on, add cooled gelatin through feed tube into avocado mixture. Chill until mixture is slightly thickened.

4. Using a mixer, whip cream. Gently fold whipped cream and avocado mixture together and turn into a 1½-quart ring mold. Chill until firm.

5. When ready to serve, unmold onto a chilled serving plate. Fill center of ring with large sprigs of watercress.

*10 to 12 servings*

# Feta Cheese Dressing

1 small clove garlic
1 package (3 ounces) cream cheese
3 ounces feta cheese
½ cup mayonnaise
½ cup half-and-half
½ teaspoon Worcestershire sauce
½ teaspoon dry mustard

Using **steel blade,** mince garlic. Add remaining ingredients and process until thoroughly blended and smooth.

# Vegetable Medley Salad Dressing

1 clove garlic
½ small cucumber
½ small avocado
1 tomato
2 tablespoons prepared horseradish
1 tablespoon sugar
1 teaspoon dry mustard
1 teaspoon paprika
½ teaspoon salt
¼ teaspoon pepper
   Few grains cayenne pepper
1 cup oil
3 tablespoons vinegar

Using **steel blade,** mince garlic. Add remaining ingredients except oil and vinegar to bowl and process a few seconds. With machine on, add the oil and vinegar through the feed tube and process until smooth.

# BREADS

# Basic White Bread

1 **package active dry yeast**
¼ **cup lukewarm water**
1¾ **cups milk, scalded**
4 **tablespoons butter**
2 **tablespoons sugar**
2 **teaspoons salt**
5½ **to 6 cups flour**
**Cornmeal**

1. Add yeast to lukewarm water and stir until dissolved and set aside.
2. In a 1-quart measuring cup, combine scalded milk, butter, sugar, and salt. Stir until completely dissolved. Cool to lukewarm; stir in the yeast mixture.
3. Aside, measure half of flour (3 cups flour). Using **steel blade,** put 2 cups flour into the bowl and add half of liquid mixture. Process a few seconds until thoroughly blended. Add remaining cup of flour, ¼ cup at a time, until dough forms into a slightly sticky, smooth ball. Once this occurs, let ball of dough spin around bowl for 20 to 30 seconds to knead the dough. Turn ball of dough onto a lightly floured board, knead by hand for a minute, and form into a neat ball.
4. Transfer to a greased bowl and rotate to coat all sides. Cover with a towel and place in a warm, draft-free place to rise for about 1½ hours, or until double in bulk.
5. Repeat procedure, using remaining ingredients.
6. When double in bulk, punch down and let rise for 30 minutes. Shape into loaves and place in greased 9×5×3-inch loaf pans, lightly sprinkled with cornmeal. Cover and let rise 45 minutes, or until double in bulk.
7. Bake at 400°F about 35 minutes.

*2 loaves bread*

# Italian Bread

1 **package active dry yeast**
2 **cups lukewarm water**
1½ **teaspoons salt**
4½ **to 5 cups flour**
**Cornmeal**

1. Add yeast to ¼ cup of lukewarm water in a small bowl. Stir until dissolved and set aside.
2. Using a 1-quart measuring cup, combine remaining 1¾ cups lukewarm water and salt. Add yeast mixture.
3. Aside, measure half of flour (2½ cups flour). Using **steel blade,** add 2 cups flour and half of water mixture to the bowl; process a few seconds until thoroughly blended. Add remaining ½ cup flour, ¼ cup at a time, until dough forms a slightly sticky smooth ball. Let dough spin in bowl for 20 to 30 seconds to knead dough. Turn dough onto a lightly floured board, knead by hand for a minute, and form into a neat ball.
4. Transfer dough to a greased bowl and rotate to coat sides. Cover with a towel and place in a warm, draft-free place to rise until double in bulk (about 2 hours).
5. Repeat procedure, using remaining ingredients.
6. When double in bulk, punch down and allow it to rise again until double in bulk (about 40 minutes). Place dough on lightly floured board, knead briefly, and make a long wide loaf. Set on a greased baking sheet, lightly sprinkled with cornmeal.
7. Cover lightly and allow to rise 30 minutes. Take a sharp razor blade and score the tops of loaves diagonally about ¼ inch deep. Let rise until double in bulk (about 30 minutes).
8. Bake at 400°F 50 minutes, or until brown and crusty. Serve warm.

*2 loaves bread*

# Cheese Bread

1 package active dry yeast
¼ cup lukewarm water
1½ cups milk, scalded
3 tablespoons vegetable shortening
1½ teaspoons salt
2 tablespoons sugar
5 ounces sharp Cheddar cheese, cut to fit feed tube
1 large carrot, pared and cut into pieces
5½ to 6 cups flour
Cornmeal

1. Add yeast to lukewarm water and stir until dissolved.
2. In a 1-quart measuring cup, combine scalded milk, shortening, salt, and sugar and stir until dissolved. Cool to lukewarm. Stir in the yeast.
3. Using **shredding disc,** shred cheese and set aside.
4. Using **steel blade,** process carrot until grated and set aside.
5. Aside, measure half of flour (3 cups flour). Using **steel blade,** put 2 cups flour, half of the shredded cheese, and half of grated carrots into the bowl and add half of liquid ingredients. Process a few seconds until thoroughly blended. Add remaining 1 cup flour, ¼ cup at a time, until dough forms into a slightly sticky, smooth ball around edge of bowl. Once this occurs, let ball of dough spin around for 20 to 30 seconds to knead the dough. Turn ball of dough onto floured bowl. Knead by hand for a minute and form into a neat ball.
6. Transfer dough to a greased bowl and rotate to coat all sides. Cover with a towel and place in a warm, draft-free place to rise for about 1½ to 2 hours, or until double in bulk.
7. Repeat procedure, using remaining flour and cheese, carrots, and liquid ingredients.
8. When double in bulk, punch down and shape into 2 loaves. Put into greased 9×5×3-inch loaf pans, lightly sprinkled with cornmeal.
9. Cover and let rise about 1½ hours, or until double in bulk.
10. Bake at 350°F about 40 minutes.

*2 loaves bread*

# Apricot Bran Bread

6 ounces dried apricots
¾ cup sugar
1½ cups whole bran cereal
1 cup milk
2 eggs
⅓ cup vegetable oil
1½ cups flour
1 tablespoon baking powder
1 teaspoon salt
1 cup raisins (optional)

1. Using **steel blade,** process dried apricots until finely chopped. Pour enough boiling water over apricots to cover; let stand for 10 minutes. Drain well and combine apricots and sugar.
2. Mix cereal and milk together and let stand until almost all of the milk is absorbed (about 2 minutes).
3. Using **plastic blade,** combine eggs and oil in the bowl and process a few seconds until well beaten. Add apricots and bran mixture and process, with quick on/off motions, until blended.
4. Combine flour, baking powder, and salt. Add dry ingredients and raisins, if desired, to the bowl and process, with quick on/off motions, until dry ingredients are incorporated into mixture.
5. Turn mixture into a greased 9×5×3-inch loaf pan and spread evenly.
6. Bake at 350°F for 65 to 70 minutes.
7. Cool bread 10 minutes in pan on wire rack; remove from pan and cool completely before slicing or storing.

*1 loaf bread*

# French Bread

2 packages active dry yeast
2½ cups warm water
1 tablespoon salt
1 tablespoon butter, melted
5½ to 6 cups flour
   Cornmeal
1 egg white
1 tablespoon cold water

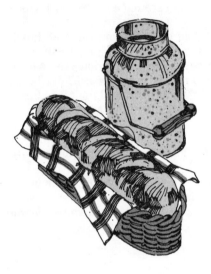

1. Sprinkle yeast over warm water in a 1-quart measuring cup. Stir until yeast is dissolved. Add salt and melted butter and thoroughly mix to dissolve salt and disperse melted butter.
2. Aside, measure half of flour (3 cups flour). With **steel blade** in the bowl, add 2 cups flour to bowl. Add half of yeast mixture to bowl and process until blended.
3. Use approximately ¾ to 1 cup more of flour, adding it ¼ cup at a time until dough forms into a fairly smooth ball. Once this occurs, let ball of dough spin in bowl for 20 to 30 seconds to thoroughly knead dough.
4. Turn dough onto lightly floured board, knead by hand for a minute, and form into a neat ball. Transfer to a greased bowl and rotate to coat all sides.
5. Cover with a towel and place in warm, draft-free place to rise until double in bulk (about 1 hour).
6. Repeat procedure, using remaining ingredients.
7. When double in bulk, punch down and turn out on a lightly floured board. Knead for a minute or two and shape into long narrow loaves. Place on a greased baking sheet lightly sprinkled with cornmeal.
8. Cover and place in a warm, draft-free place to rise again until double in bulk (about 1 hour). Using a sharp razor blade, score surface with 3 diagonal cuts, ¼ inch deep. Brush lightly with egg white mixed with 1 tablespoon cold water.
9. Bake at 400°F 55 minutes, or until crusty and golden brown.

*2 long loaves bread*

*Note:* For added crustiness, place a pan of hot water on bottom of oven. Also, during first few minutes of baking, gently spray loaves with a fine mist of water.

# Russian Black Bread

2 cups rye flour
2 cups all-purpose flour
¼ cup unsweetened cocoa
1½ teaspoons instant coffee
2 tablespoons caraway seed
1 package active dry yeast
1¼ cups lukewarm water
2 tablespoons sugar
1 teaspoon salt
2 tablespoons vinegar
3 tablespoons dark molasses
2 tablespoons melted butter
   Cornmeal

1. Using **steel blade,** add flours, cocoa, coffee, and caraway seed to bowl and process a few seconds until thoroughly combined. Remove from bowl and set aside.
2. In a 1-quart measuring cup, dissolve yeast in lukewarm water and let stand for 10 minutes until foamy.
3. Add sugar, salt, vinegar, molasses, and melted butter to yeast mixture and stir until salt and sugar are dissolved.
4. Aside, measure half of flour mixture (approximately 2 cups flour). Using **steel blade,** add 1½ cups flour to the bowl. With machine on, add half of liquid ingredients through the feed tube and process a few seconds until thoroughly blended. Add remaining ½ cup flour ¼ cup at a time until the dough forms into a slightly sticky, smooth ball around the edge of the bowl. Once this occurs, let the ball of dough spin around for 20 to 30 seconds to thoroughly knead the dough. Turn the

ball of dough onto a lightly floured board and knead for about 1 minute by hand, and form into a neat ball.

5. Repeat procedure, using remaining ingredients. Combine two balls into one to make one large loaf.

6. Transfer ball of dough to a greased bowl and rotate to coat all sides. Cover with a damp cloth and place in a warm, draft-free place to rise until double in bulk (about 1 hour).

7. Punch down dough. Turn onto a lightly floured board and shape into a ball. Place ball of dough in the center of a greased 9-inch round cake pan lightly sprinkled with cornmeal. Cover and put in a warm, draft-free place to rise until double in bulk (about 1 hour).

8. Bake at 350°F 40 to 45 minutes, or until done.

*1 large round loaf*

# Greek Sesame Bread

2 **packages active dry yeast**
1 **cup lukewarm water**
1 **cup milk, scalded**
3 **tablespoons sugar**
1 **tablespoon salt**
4 **tablespoons butter, cut in pieces**
1 **egg**
5½ **to 6 cups flour**
  **Cornmeal**
2 **tablespoons half-and-half**
3 **tablespoons sesame seed**

1. Add yeast to lukewarm water and stir until dissolved.

2. In a 1-quart measuring cup, combine scalded milk, sugar, salt, and butter and stir until dissolved. Cool to lukewarm.

3. Using **steel blade,** lightly beat egg. Add egg and yeast mixture to cooled milk mixture.

4. Aside, measure half of flour (3 cups flour). Using **steel blade,** put 2 cups of flour into the bowl and add half of liquid ingredients. Process a few seconds until thoroughly blended. Add remaining cup of flour, ¼ cup at a time, until dough forms into a slightly sticky, smooth ball around edge of bowl, usually after 2½ to 2¾ cups flour. Let ball of dough spin around bowl for 20 to 30 seconds to knead the dough. Turn ball of dough onto floured board, knead for a minute by hand, and form into a neat ball.

5. Transfer dough to a greased bowl and rotate to coat all sides. Cover with a towel and place in a warm, draft-free place to rise for 1½ to 2 hours, or until double in bulk.

6. Repeat procedure, using remaining flour and liquid ingredients. Combine two balls of dough only if making one large loaf.

7. When double in bulk, punch down and turn dough onto lightly floured board; form into ball again. Place each ball of dough into a well-greased 9-inch round cake pan, lightly sprinkled with cornmeal.

8. Brush each loaf with half-and-half and sprinkle with sesame seed. Cover and put into a warm, draft-free place to rise for 1½ to 2 hours.

9. Bake at 350°F for 40 minutes, or until loaves are crusty.

*Two 9-inch round loaves*

# Irish Sweet Bread

1 package active dry yeast
¾ cup lukewarm water
¾ cup milk, scalded
⅓ cup shortening
2 teaspoons salt
½ cup sugar
1 teaspoon grated lemon peel
½ teaspoon almond extract
2 eggs
5½ to 6 cups flour
1 egg white
1 tablespoon cold water

1. Add yeast to lukewarm water and stir until dissolved. Set aside.
2. In a 1-quart measuring cup, combine milk, shortening, salt, sugar, lemon peel, and almond extract. Stir until dissolved. Cool to lukewarm and add yeast mixture.
3. Using **steel blade,** add eggs to bowl and beat lightly. Add eggs to liquid ingredients.
4. Aside, measure half of flour (3 cups flour). Using **steel blade,** put 2 cups flour in the bowl and add half of liquid ingredients. Process a few seconds until thoroughly blended. Add remaining 1 cup of flour, ¼ cup at a time, until dough forms into a slightly sticky, smooth ball, usually after 2¾ cups flour. Once this occurs, let ball of dough spin around bowl for 20 to 30 seconds to thoroughly knead the dough.
5. Turn ball of dough onto a lightly floured board, knead for a minute by hand and form into a neat ball.
6. Transfer dough to a greased bowl and rotate to coat all sides. Cover with a towel and place in a warm, draft-free place to rise about 2 hours, or until double in bulk.
7. Repeat procedure, using remaining flour and liquid ingredients.
8. When double in bulk, punch down and let rise again for about 2 hours, or until double in bulk.
9. Divide each ball of dough into 3 equal pieces. Roll each piece into a uniformly even 12-inch cylinder. Braid the three rolls together. Place in a greased 9×5×3-inch loaf. Cover and let rise 30 minutes.
10. Brush lightly with egg white mixed with the cold water.
11. Bake at 350°F for about 30 minutes, or until bread tests done.

*2 loaves bread*

# Vesta's Currant Bread

1 package active dry yeast
¼ cup lukewarm water
1¼ cups milk, scalded
¾ cup sugar
2 teaspoons salt
5 tablespoons vegetable shortening
2 eggs, lightly beaten
½ teaspoon nutmeg
½ teaspoon mace
5½ to 6 cups flour
2 cups currants

1. Add yeast to lukewarm water and stir until dissolved. Set aside.
2. In a 1-quart measuring cup, combine scalded milk, sugar, salt, and shortening. Stir to dissolve salt and sugar and to melt shortening; cool to lukewarm.
3. Using **steel blade,** add eggs, nutmeg, and mace to the bowl and process until eggs are lightly beaten. Add eggs and yeast to milk mixture in measuring cup.
4. Aside, measure half of flour (3 cups flour). Using **steel blade,** put 2 cups flour in the bowl and add half of liquid ingredients. Process a few seconds until thoroughly blended. Add remaining cup of flour, ¼ cup at a time, and process until dough forms into a slightly sticky, smooth ball of dough, usually after 2¾ cups flour. Once this occurs, let ball of dough spin around bowl for 20 to 30 seconds to thoroughly knead the dough. Turn ball of dough onto a lightly floured board, knead by hand for a minute and form into a ball.
5. Transfer dough to a greased bowl and rotate to coat all

sides. Cover with a damp towel and place in a warm, draft-free place to rise for about 2 hours, or until double in bulk.

6. Repeat procedure, using remaining flour and liquid ingredients.

7. When double in bulk, punch down and turn onto a lightly floured board. Roll each ball of dough into a rectangle 20×9-inches. Sprinkle half of currants over dough and roll up tightly in jelly-roll fashion. Tuck the ends under and place, seam side down, in a well-greased 9×5×3-inch loaf pan.

8. Cover and place in a warm, draft-free place to rise 1½ hours, or until double in bulk.

9. Bake at 325°F 1¼ hours, or until loaves are done.

*2 loaves bread*

# Eunice's Anadama Bread

1½ cups water
1½ teaspoons salt
⅓ cup yellow cornmeal
⅓ cup light molasses
1½ tablespoons shortening
¼ cup lukewarm water
1 package active dry yeast
4 to 4½ cups flour
Cornmeal

1. In a saucepan, combine 1½ cups water and salt and bring to a boil. Stir in cornmeal and return to a boil, stirring constantly. Immediately remove from heat and stir in molasses and shortening. Cool to lukewarm.

2. Add yeast to lukewarm water and stir until dissolved. Set aside.

3. When cornmeal mixture has cooled, combine it with yeast in a 1-quart measuring cup.

4. Aside, measure half of flour (2¼ cups flour). Using **steel blade,** add 1¾ cups flour to the bowl and add half of cornmeal mixture. Process a few seconds until thoroughly blended. Add remaining ½ cup flour, ¼ cup at a time, until dough forms into a slightly sticky, smooth ball around the edge of bowl, usually after 2¼ cups flour. Once this occurs, let ball of dough spin around for 20 to 30 seconds to thoroughly knead the dough. Turn ball of dough onto a lightly floured board, knead by hand a minute, and form into a neat ball.

5. Transfer dough to a greased bowl and rotate to coat all sides. Cover with a damp towel and place in a warm, draft-free place to rise for about 1½ hours, or until dough is double in bulk.

6. Repeat procedure, using remaining flour and liquid ingredients. Combine two balls of dough if making one large loaf.

7. When double in bulk, punch down and turn onto a lightly floured board and form into a loaf. For 1 large loaf, place in a well-greased 9×5×3-inch loaf pan, lightly sprinkled with cornmeal. For 2 smaller loaves, place in two well-greased 8×4×2-inch loaf pans.

8. Brush tops with melted butter and sprinkle with cornmeal. Cover and place in a warm, draft-free place to rise for 1 hour, or until double in bulk again.

9. Bake at 375°F 40 to 45 minutes, or until bread sounds hollow when thumped.

*1 large or 2 small loaves*

# Spiral Herb Bread

2 packages active dry yeast
1 cup lukewarm water
1 cup milk, scalded
4 tablespoons butter
3 tablespoons sugar
2 teaspoons salt
5½ to 6 cups flour
1 clove garlic
2 cups fresh parsley
1 cup fresh chives (or ¼ cup dried)
½ cup fresh dill (or 2 tablespoons dried)
2 tablespoons tarragon
2 tablespoons chervil

1. Add yeast to lukewarm water and stir until dissolved. Set aside.
2. In a 1-quart measuring cup, combine milk, butter, sugar, and salt and stir until dissolved. Cool to lukewarm and add yeast mixture.
3. Aside, measure half of flour (3 cups flour). Using **steel blade,** put 2 cups flour in the bowl and add half of liquid ingredients. Process a few seconds until thoroughly blended. Add remaining cup of flour, ¼ cup at a time, until dough forms into a slightly sticky, smooth ball, usually after 2¾ cups flour. Once this occurs, let ball of dough spin around bowl for 20 to 30 seconds to thoroughly knead the dough. Turn ball of dough onto a lightly floured board, knead by hand for a minute, and form into a neat ball.
4. Transfer dough to a greased bowl and rotate to coat all sides. Cover with a towel and place in a warm, draft-free place to rise for 1 hour, or until double in bulk.
5. Repeat procedure, using remaining flour and liquid ingredients.
6. When double in bulk, punch down and turn onto a lightly floured board. Roll each ball of dough into a rectangle 20×9-inches.
7. Using **steel blade,** mince garlic. Add parsley and remaining ingredients to bowl and process until finely chopped.
8. Spread half of herb mixture over dough and roll up tightly in a jelly-roll fashion. Tuck the ends under and place seam side down in a well-greased 9×5×3-inch loaf pan.
9. Cover and place in a warm, draft-free place to rise 1 hour, or until double in bulk.
10. Bake at 400°F 1 hour.

*2 loaves bread*

# Graham Date Bread

2½ packages graham crackers (about 40), broken in quarters (3 cups crumbs)
1 cup walnuts
¾ cup flour
¾ cup sugar
3½ teaspoons baking powder
¾ teaspoon salt
2 eggs
1 cup milk
¼ cup salad oil
1 teaspoon vanilla extract
1 package (7 ounces) chopped dates

1. Using **steel blade,** separately process graham crackers to fine powder and walnuts until coarsely chopped. Set aside.
2. Combine dry ingredients and graham cracker crumbs and mix together. This can be done quickly in the food processor with **steel blade.** Set aside.
3. Using **steel blade,** add eggs to the bowl and process until lightly beaten. Add milk, salad oil, and vanilla extract and process until thoroughly blended. Remove from bowl.
4. Still using **steel blade,** add half of graham cracker crumb mixture, all of liquids, remainder of graham cracker crumbs, walnuts, and dates and process only until dry ingredients are incorporated into mixture.
5. Turn into a well-greased 9×5×3-inch loaf pan and spread evenly.
6. Bake at 350°F about 65 minutes, or until bread tests done. Cool 10 minutes before removing from pan. Cool completely before serving.

*1 loaf bread*

**From the German dinner menu on page 8: Walnut Torte, 70**

# Cloverleaf Rolls

2 packages active dry yeast
¼ cup lukewarm water
1 cup milk
8 tablespoons butter (1 stick), cut in 5 pieces
½ cup sugar
1 teaspoon salt
2 eggs
5 cups flour
¼ cup melted butter

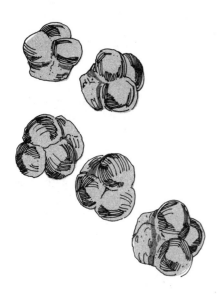

1. Add yeast to lukewarm water and stir until dissolved; set aside to cool.
2. Scald milk, remove from heat, and add butter, sugar, and salt; stir to dissolve. Cool to lukewarm.
3. Using **steel blade,** beat eggs until frothy.
4. In a 1-quart measuring cup, combine yeast mixture, milk mixture, and beaten eggs and stir thoroughly.
5. Aside, measure half of flour (2½ cups). Using **steel blade,** add 2 cups flour and half of liquid ingredients; process until blended.
6. Add remaining ½ cup of flour, ¼ cup at a time, and process until dough forms itself into a fairly smooth ball. Then let ball of dough spin around the bowl for about 20 to 30 seconds to thoroughly knead the dough.
7. Turn dough onto lightly floured board, knead by hand for a minute, and form into a neat ball. Transfer to a greased bowl and rotate to coat all sides.
8. Cover with a damp cloth and place in a warm, draft-free place to rise until double in bulk (about 1½ hours).
9. Repeat procedure, using remaining ingredients.
10. When double in bulk, punch the dough down. Let it rest for 15 minutes. Break off dough and form into balls the size of a walnut.
11. Roll each ball in melted butter.
12. Grease muffin-pan wells and place 3 balls in bottom of each well.
13. Cover loosely with a towel and let rise again in a warm, draft-free place until doubled in bulk (about 1 hour).
14. Bake at 400°F about 15 minutes. Serve warm.

*36 rolls*

# Green Chili Cornbread

4 ounces sharp Cheddar cheese (2 cups shredded)
2 green onions, trimmed and cut in 1-inch pieces
1 can (4 ounces) whole green chilies, drained and seeded
1 cup milk
1 egg
¼ cup vegetable oil
1¼ cups cornmeal
¾ cup flour
¼ cup sugar
1 tablespoon baking powder
½ teaspoon salt
1 can (8 ounces) whole kernel corn

1. Using **shredding disc,** shred cheese and set aside.
2. Using **steel blade,** process the green onions until finely chopped.
3. Add green chilies to green onions in bowl and process, in quick on/off motions, until finely chopped and set aside.
4. With **plastic blade** in bowl, add milk, egg, and oil, and process until blended. Add cornmeal, flour, sugar, baking powder, and salt and mix together for a few seconds. Add corn, green onions, and chilies.
5. Pour half of batter into a greased 9-inch square baking pan. Sprinkle with half of cheese. Repeat, using remaining batter and cheese.
6. Bake at 400°F about 35 to 40 minutes, or until lightly browned. Serve warm cut in squares.

*8 to 12 servings*

**From the French dinner menu on page 8:**
**Raspberry Mousse, 92**

# Golden Orange-Nut Bread

½ cup walnuts
1 medium orange
2½ cups flour
1 tablespoon baking powder
¾ cup sugar
½ teaspoon baking soda
1 teaspoon salt
1 egg
Buttermilk (about ⅔ cup)
3 tablespoons shortening, melted and cooled
1 cup golden raisins

1. Using **steel blade,** process walnuts until coarsely chopped. Set aside.
2. Cut orange in half. Squeeze out juice and set juice aside. Discard any seeds. Cut orange halves into quarters. Using **steel blade,** process orange pieces until finely chopped. Set aside.
3. Combine dry ingredients and mix together.
4. Using **steel blade,** process egg until frothy.
5. Measure reserved orange juice and add enough buttermilk to make 1 cup liquid. Add with melted shortening to bowl and process until thoroughly blended. Remove from bowl.
6. Still using **steel blade,** add half of dry ingredients, all of orange juice-buttermilk mixture, other half of dry ingredients, chopped orange, and then raisins. Process, using quick on/off motions, until dry ingredients are incorporated into mixture.
7. Turn into a well-greased 9×5×3-inch loaf pan and spread evenly.
8. Bake at 350°F about 1¼ hours, or until bread tests done.
9. Cool 10 minutes on a wire rack. Remove loaf from pan and cool completely.

*1 loaf bread*

*Note:* The flavor of this bread improves on standing one day. It is an excellent bread to slice thinly and spread with cream cheese.

# Carrot Bread

2 large carrots, pared and cut in 1-inch pieces
1 cup sugar
¾ cup salad oil
2 eggs
1¾ cups flour
1 teaspoon cinnamon
½ teaspoon nutmeg
1 teaspoon baking powder
½ teaspoon baking soda
¾ teaspoon salt
1 cup raisins

1. Using **steel blade,** process carrots until grated and remove from bowl.
2. Still using **steel blade,** combine sugar and oil in bowl and process until smooth and well blended.
3. Add finely grated carrots and eggs, one at a time, blending well after each addition.
4. Add dry ingredients and process, with quick on/off motions, until blended together. Add raisins and process only until raisins are incorporated into mixture.
5. Pour batter into a greased and floured 9×5×3-inch loaf pan.
6. Bake at 350°F 1 hour.

*1 loaf bread*

# DESSERTS

# Chocolate Pound Cake

1¾ cups flour
1 teaspoon baking powder
⅛ teaspoon salt
¼ cup cocoa
¾ cup butter
1½ teaspoons vanilla extract
¼ teaspoon almond extract
1½ cups sugar
3 eggs
⅔ cup milk

1. In a bowl, combine flour, baking powder, salt, and cocoa and mix together. Set aside.
2. Using **steel blade,** put butter in the bowl and process until creamy. Add extracts. With machine on, add sugar gradually through the feed tube. Add eggs, one at a time, and process until fluffy.
3. With machine on, add milk through feed tube. Add dry ingredients and process, using quick on/off motions, until flour is incorporated into mixture.
4. Turn batter into greased 9×5×3-inch loaf pan and spread batter evenly.
5. Bake at 325°F about 65 minutes, or until cake tests done.
6. Cool cake in pan for 15 minutes before removing from pan. Let cake cool completely before serving.

*1 loaf cake*

# Upside-down Passover Prune Cake

**Cake:**
2 jars (16 ounces each) cooked dried prunes
6 eggs, separated
1 cup sugar
1 teaspoon grated lemon peel
1 tablespoon lemon juice
½ teaspoon salt
¾ cup matzo cake meal

**Prune Sauce:**
Reserved prune juice
2 teaspoons potato starch
¼ cup sugar
1 teaspoon grated lemon peel
3 tablespoons lemon juice

1. For cake, drain prunes, reserving 6 tablespoons of liquid for sauce. Pit and drain on paper towels.
2. Using **steel blade,** add egg yolks, sugar, lemon peel, lemon juice, and salt to the bowl; process until very thick. Add cake meal and process, with quick on/off motions, until incorporated (this will be a very heavy consistency). Turn into a bowl.
3. Using a mixer, beat egg whites until stiff, but not dry. Fold a fourth of egg whites into egg yolk mixture to lighten it. Then gently add remaining egg whites into egg mixture.
4. Generously grease a 9-inch tubed springform pan and line bottom with waxed paper. Arrange about half of the prunes on the paper.
5. Turn batter into pan over prunes and spread evenly.
6. Bake at 350°F about 40 minutes, or until cake is browned and firm to touch. Remove the springform and cool cake completely.
7. Meanwhile, for sauce, blend prune juice with potato starch in a small saucepan. Mix in remaining ingredients. Cook and stir over low heat until thickened.
8. Invert cooled cake onto plate, remove bottom of pan, and carefully peel off paper. Spoon Prune Sauce over cake and place remaining prunes around cake. Serve with Orange Buttercream.

*One 9-inch tube cake*

## Orange Buttercream

8 tablespoons butter, softened
2 teaspoons grated orange peel
2 egg yolks
¾ cup confectioners' sugar
1 teaspoon curacao (optional)

1. Using **steel blade,** cream butter with orange peel.
2. Add remaining ingredients and process until creamy. More or less sugar can be added to reach desired consistency. Spoon into a serving dish.

# Orange Crumb Coffee Cake

**Cake:**
- 2 eggs
- 8 tablespoons butter (1 stick), softened and cut in 6 pieces
- ½ cup sugar
- ⅓ cup firmly packed brown sugar
- 2 teaspoons grated orange peel
- ½ cup orange juice
- ½ cup milk
- 2 teaspoons vanilla extract
- 2 cups flour
- 1 tablespoon baking powder
- ⅛ teaspoon salt

**Topping:**
- ⅓ cup sugar
- ⅓ cup flour
- 3 tablespoons butter, frozen and cut in 3 pieces
- 2 teaspoons grated orange peel

1. For cake, using **steel blade,** process eggs until frothy and remove from bowl.
2. Using **steel blade,** process butter, sugars, and orange peel until thoroughly blended and fluffy. Add eggs and process until smooth and well blended.
3. Add orange juice, milk, and vanilla extract and process until creamy.
4. Mix dry ingredients and add to bowl; process for 5 seconds, stop to scrape down sides, and process 5 seconds more until flour is incorporated and mixture is smooth.
5. Pour batter into a greased 9-inch square pan.
6. For topping, using **steel blade,** add all ingredients to bowl and process, using quick on/off motions, until crumbly. Sprinkle topping over cake.
7. Bake at 350°F about 45 to 50 minutes, or until cake tests done.

*One 9-inch square cake*

# Chocolate-Ricotta Cheese Cake

**Pastry Dough:**
- 2 cups flour
- ½ cup sugar
- 7 tablespoons soft butter
- 3 tablespoons shortening
- 3 egg yolks
- 1 whole egg
- 1 teaspoon grated lemon peel

**Filling:**
- ½ cup uncooked rice
- 2 ounces (2 squares) unsweetened chocolate
- 1 pound ricotta cheese
- 1½ cups sugar
- 1 teaspoon grated lemon peel
- 3 egg yolks
- ¼ teaspoon cinnamon
- 1 teaspoon vanilla extract
- 2 egg whites

1. For pastry dough, using **steel blade,** put all ingredients into the bowl and process until thoroughly blended.
2. Place two thirds of dough in a 9-inch springform pan. Using your fingers, spread it carefully over bottom and approximately 1½ inches up the sides. Chill shell and remaining dough while preparing filling.
3. For filling, cook rice, rinse it with cold water, and set aside to cool.
4. Melt chocolate in a double boiler and cool.
5. Using **steel blade,** add ricotta to the bowl and process until smooth. Add 1 cup sugar, grated lemon peel, egg yolks, cinnamon, the melted chocolate, and vanilla extract; process until creamy.
6. Using a mixer, beat 2 egg whites with remaining ½ cup sugar until stiff. Add to ricotta mixture and fold together. Fold in cooked rice.
7. Pour filling into pan. Roll out remaining dough on a floured board. Cut into 1-inch strips and arrange in lattice fashion on top.
8. Bake at 350°F 1 hour and 10 minutes, or until cake is firm and lattice is golden. Cool before serving.

*One 9-inch cheese cake*

# German Chocolate Cheese Cake

**Crust:**
- 15 **graham crackers, broken in quarters**
- 6 **tablespoons butter, cut in 6 pieces**
- ¼ **cup confectioners' sugar**

**Filling:**
- 6 **ounces sweet chocolate**
- 4 **packages (8 ounces) cream cheese, cut in quarters**
- 5 **eggs**
- 1 **cup sugar**
- 1 **tablespoon vanilla extract**

**Topping:**
- ½ **cup pecans**
- 2 **tablespoons butter**
- ⅓ **cup light cream**
- 2 **tablespoons brown sugar**
- 1 **egg**
- ½ **teaspoon vanilla extract**
- ½ **cup grated coconut**
  **Whipped cream and chocolate shavings for garnish**

1. For crust, using **steel blade,** process graham crackers to fine crumbs. Add butter and confectioners' sugar and process until thoroughly blended. Pat into bottom and part way up sides of a 10-inch springform pan. Bake at 350°F 10 minutes. Lower heat to 325°F for cake.

2. For filling, melt chocolate in a double boiler and cool slightly.

3. Using **steel blade,** process 1 package of cream cheese and 1 egg until smooth. Add another package of cream cheese and another egg and process until smooth. Repeat 2 more times, using remaining cream cheese and eggs. Lastly, add sugar and vanilla extract and process until smooth and creamy.

4. Pour into prepared crust and bake at 325°F 1 hour, or until firm in the center. Cool on a rack at room temperature.

5. For topping, using **steel blade,** process pecans, with quick on/off motions, until chopped. Set aside.

6. Combine butter, cream, brown sugar, and egg in a small saucepan. Cook over medium heat until thick, stirring constantly. Remove from heat and stir in vanilla extract, coconut, and chopped pecans. Cool.

7. Remove sides from springform pan. Top with pecan topping to within 1 inch of edge. Decorate with a border of whipped cream. Sprinkle chocolate shavings over the top.

*10 to 12 servings*

# Linda's Favorite Cheese Cake

**Crust:**
- 1 **cup flour**
- ¼ **cup sugar**
- 1 **teaspoon grated lemon peel**
- ½ **teaspoon vanilla extract**
- 8 **tablespoons butter, cut in 6 pieces**
- 1 **egg yolk**

**Filling:**
- 4 **packages (8 ounces each) cream cheese, cut in quarters**
- 5 **eggs**
- 1¼ **cups sugar**
- 3 **tablespoons flour**
- 1 **teaspoon grated lemon peel**

1. For crust, using **steel blade,** place all ingredients in the bowl and process until mixture is thoroughly blended. Using your hands, pat onto bottom and sides of a 9-inch springform pan.

2. Bake at 400°F 10 to 15 minutes, or until lightly browned.

3. For filling, using **steel blade,** add 1 package cream cheese and 1 egg to the bowl and process until smooth. Add another package of cream cheese and another egg and process until smooth. Add last package of cream cheese and another egg and process until smooth. Add last two eggs and remainder of ingredients and process until smooth and creamy.

4. Pour cheese mixture into baked crust.

5. Bake at 325°F 1 hour, or until firm. Cool and top with Strawberry Glaze.

1 teaspoon grated orange peel
½ teaspoon vanilla extract

**Strawberry Glaze:**
1 quart strawberries
½ cup sugar
1½ tablespoons cornstarch
Dash salt
1 teaspoon butter

6. For glaze, wash and hull strawberries. Set enough whole, large, perfect strawberries aside to cover top of cheese cake. Using **steel blade,** process enough small, uneven strawberries to make 1 cup of puree. Put through a sieve.
7. In a saucepan, combine strawberry puree, sugar, cornstarch, and salt. Bring to boiling, stirring constantly; boil for 2 minutes, stirring occasionally. Stir in butter and cool slightly.
8. Arrange whole strawberries on top of cooled cheese cake. Spoon glaze over the berries. Or chill cheese cake and glaze separately; then serve glaze as a sauce. Chill before serving.
*10 to 12 servings*

*Note:* Glaze can also be made with canned blueberries or canned crushed pineapple. Drain fruit, reserving juice. Add fruit and ½ cup juice to saucepan. Combine with ¼ cup sugar, cornstarch, and salt. Follow above instructions. Cook until thickened and cool. Spoon over cooled cheese cake and chill.

# Honey-Cheese Pie

**Pastry Dough:**
1½ cups flour
1½ teaspoons baking powder
½ teaspoon salt
2 tablespoons sugar
8 tablespoons butter (1 stick), frozen and cut in 6 pieces
¼ cup ice water

**Filling:**
3 packages (8 ounces each) cream cheese, cut in quarters
6 eggs
¾ cup sugar
¾ cup honey
2 teaspoons cinnamon

1. For dough, using **steel blade,** put flour, baking powder, salt, sugar, and butter into bowl. Process until crumbly and butter is cut into flour.
2. With machine on, add ice water through feed tube and process until dough forms into a ball.
3. Roll out dough and line a 10-inch pie plate; flute pastry edge.
4. For filling, using **steel blade,** add 1 package of cream cheese and 2 eggs to the bowl. Process until smooth. Add another package of cream cheese and 2 more eggs and process until smooth. Add remaining cream cheese and eggs and process. Add sugar, honey, and cinnamon and process until creamy.
5. Pour mixture into lined pie plate.
6. Bake at 350°F about 1 hour, or until golden brown. Serve warm or cooled.
*12 servings*

# Old-fashioned Gingerbread

½ cup butter
½ cup sugar
1 egg
1 cup dark molasses
3 cups flour
1½ teaspoons baking soda
½ teaspoon salt
1 teaspoon cinnamon
1 teaspoon ginger
½ teaspoon cloves
1¼ cups boiling water

1. Using **steel blade,** process butter until light and fluffy. Gradually add sugar through feed tube. Add egg and molasses; process until well blended.
2. Combine dry ingredients.
3. With machine on, add boiling water through feed tube to sugar mixture; process a few seconds until blended. Add dry ingredients, using quick on/off motions, only until flour is totally incorporated into mixture.
4. Pour mixture into a well-greased 9×9×2-inch pan.
5. Bake at 350°F about 45 minutes, or until top springs back when lightly touched. Serve warm with **whipped cream.**
*9 servings*

# Apricot Squares

8 tablespoons butter (1 stick), cut in
    6 pieces
¼ cup sugar
1⅓ cups flour
½ cup walnuts
1 package (6 ounces) dried apricots
½ teaspoon baking powder
¼ teaspoon salt
2 eggs
1 cup firmly packed brown sugar
½ teaspoon vanilla extract
    Confectioners' sugar

1. Using **steel blade,** add butter, sugar, and 1 cup flour to bowl and process until mixture is blended and forms into a ball. Pat into a greased 9×9×2-inch pan. Bake at 350°F for 25 minutes.
2. Using **steel blade,** process walnuts, using quick on/off motions, until coarsely chopped. Set aside.
3. Using **steel blade,** add dried apricots to bowl and process until finely chopped. Transfer to a saucepan, cover with water, and boil for 10 minutes. Drain thoroughly and cool.
4. Combine remaining ⅓ cup flour, baking powder, and salt.
5. Using **plastic blade,** add eggs to bowl and process until frothy. Gradually add brown sugar through the feed tube, processing until thoroughly blended and creamy. Add flour mixture, chopped walnuts, chopped apricots, and vanilla extract and process, using quick on/off motions, until flour is incorporated and mixture is blended. Spread over baked layer.
6. Bake at 350°F about 35 minutes, or until done. Cool in pan and cut into small squares. Sprinkle with confectioners' sugar.

*About 2 dozen squares*

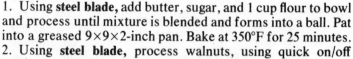

# Marble Squares

*Cheese Mixture:*
1 package (8 ounces) cream cheese,
    quartered
⅓ cup sugar
1 egg
½ teaspoon vanilla extract

*Cookie Mixture:*
8 tablespoons butter, cut in pieces
¾ cup water
1½ ounces (1½ squares) unsweetened
    chocolate
2 eggs
2 cups sugar
½ cup dairy sour cream
2 cups flour
1 teaspoon baking soda
½ teaspoon salt
1 package (6 ounces) semisweet
    chocolate pieces

1. For cheese mixture, using **steel blade,** add all ingredients to the bowl and process until creamy and smooth. Remove from bowl and set aside.

2. For cookie mixture, combine butter, water, and chocolate in a saucepan and bring to boiling. Stir until chocolate is melted and remove from heat.
3. Using **steel blade,** add eggs, sugar, and sour cream to bowl and process until thoroughly blended. Add chocolate mixture and process until smooth, stopping to scrape down the sides.
4. Mix dry ingredients and add to bowl with egg mixture. Process, with quick on/off motions, until flour is incorporated into mixture.
5. Pour into a greased and floured 15×10×1-inch jelly-roll pan.
6. Spoon cream-cheese mixture over the chocolate batter and swirl with a spoon to get a marbled effect. Sprinkle the chocolate pieces over the top.
7. Bake at 375°F 25 to 30 minutes. Let cool slightly and cut into squares.

*5 to 6 dozen cookies*

# Rolled French Cookies

**Cookies:**
  3 tablespoons butter, softened and
     cut in 2 pieces
  1 teaspoon grated lemon or orange
     peel
  ⅓ cup sugar
  1 egg
  ¼ teaspoon vanilla extract
  ⅓ cup flour

**Chocolate Buttercream Filling:**
  4 ounces sweet chocolate
  2 tablespoons coffee
  8 tablespoons butter (1 stick),
     softened and cut in 6 pieces
  1 cup confectioners' sugar
  1 tablespoon curacao (or any other
     orange liqueur)

1. For cookies, using **steel blade,** process butter until smooth. With machine on, add lemon peel and sugar gradually through the feed tube and process until fluffy.
2. Add egg and vanilla extract and process until creamy yellow.
3. Add flour and process a few seconds. Stop and scrape down sides of bowl and process a few seconds more.
4. Drop by teaspoonfuls onto an oiled baking sheet. Place only 9 cookies on a sheet, as they spread out when cooked.
5. Bake at 400°F about 5 minutes, or until edges of cookies are golden brown.
6. To form cookies into rolls or cigarettes, roll them around a sharpening steel immediately after coming out of the oven. Do *not* let them cool, as they will crumble. If the entire tray of cookies cannot be rolled before the last ones cool, place the tray back in the oven for a minute or so. These cookies require a little patience at first, but they are well worth the effort.
7. For filling, melt chocolate with coffee in a double boiler and cool.
8. Using **plastic blade,** process butter until creamy. Add chocolate, confectioners' sugar, and curacao and process until thoroughly blended.
9. Put filling in a pastry bag and fill rolled cookies. Chill to firm filling.

*About 18 cookies*

# Almond Cookies

  65 almonds, blanched
  2½ cups flour
  2 eggs
  ½ cup butter
  ½ cup shortening
  1 cup sugar
  2 teaspoons almond extract
  ½ teaspoon baking soda
  ⅛ teaspoon salt
  1 egg yolk beaten with 1 tablespoon
     water for glaze

1. Set 40 whole almonds aside. Using **shredding disc,** shred remaining almonds. Remove shredding disc and insert **steel blade.** Add 1 cup flour to shredded nuts and process to a fine powder. Remove from bowl.
2. Using **steel blade,** process eggs until lightly beaten and remove from bowl.
3. Using **steel blade,** cream butter, shortening, and sugar together until smooth. Add eggs and almond extract and process until blended.
4. Combine remaining 1½ cups flour, baking soda, and salt. Add flour mixture and powdered almonds to bowl and process only until blended.
5. Form dough into balls the size of a walnut. Place on a cookie sheet greased with peanut oil. Flatten cookies with the bottom of a glass dipped in flour. Brush each cookie with egg-yolk glaze. Place whole almond in the center of each cookie.
6. Bake at 350°F 15 to 20 minutes.

*About 40 cookies*

# Lemon-Raisin Crisscross Cookies

4 tablespoons butter, cut into 3 pieces
¼ cup vegetable shortening
¾ cup sugar
1 egg
2 tablespoons grated lemon peel
1 tablespoon lemon juice
1¾ cups flour
¾ teaspoon cream of tartar
¾ teaspoon baking soda
¼ teaspoon salt
1 cup raisins

1. Using **steel blade,** process butter, shortening, sugar, egg, lemon peel, and lemon juice until light and fluffy.
2. In a bowl, combine dry ingredients and mix together.
3. Add dry ingredients and raisins to the bowl and process, using quick on/off motions, until flour is incorporated into mixture.
4. Shape the dough into walnut-size balls. Place on a greased cookie sheet. Flatten balls in a crisscross pattern with a fork dipped in sugar.
5. Bake at 400°F 8 to 10 minutes.

*3 dozen cookies*

# Walnut Torte

10 ounces walnuts (3½ cups grated)
½ cup flour
½ teaspoon instant coffee
½ teaspoon cocoa
6 eggs, separated
1 cup sugar
1 teaspoon grated lemon peel
1 teaspoon vanilla extract
Mocha Butter Frosting

1. Grease bottoms of two 8-inch round layer cake pans. Line bottoms with waxed paper and grease waxed paper. Set aside.
2. Using **shredding disc,** shred walnuts. Set ¾ cup walnuts aside. Remove shredding disc and insert **steel blade.** Add flour, coffee, and cocoa to bowl and process remaining walnuts to a fine powder. Remove from bowl and set aside.
3. Using **steel blade,** process egg yolks, ½ cup sugar, and lemon peel until very thick and lemon colored (about 2 to 3 minutes). Add vanilla extract and process until blended.
4. Using a mixer, beat egg whites until frothy. Gradually add ½ cup sugar, beating well after each addition. Beat until rounded peaks are formed and egg whites do not slide when bowl is tipped. Gently spread egg-yolk mixture over beaten egg whites. Spoon a fourth of flour-walnut mixture over egg mixture and gently fold with a few strokes until batter is only partially blended. Repeat with second, third, and fourth portions and fold until just blended. Do not overmix!
5. Gently turn batter into prepared pans.
6. Bake at 350°F 25 to 30 minutes, or until torte tests done. Cool before removing from pan. Run spatula gently around sides of pan. Cover with wire rack. Invert and remove pan. Remove waxed paper and turn right side up.
7. Fill layers with frosting. Frost top and sides of cake and sprinkle top with remaining chopped walnuts. Chill to firm frosting.

*One 8-inch torte*

## Mocha Butter Frosting

4 ounces sweet chocolate
1 tablespoon instant coffee
2 tablespoons water
¾ cup butter
½ cup confectioners' sugar

1. In the top of a double boiler, melt chocolate with coffee and water. Remove from heat and cool.
2. Using **steel blade,** cream butter. Add cooled chocolate mixture and confectioners' sugar. Process until smooth.

# Chocolate Carrot Torte

**Torte:**
- 4 ounces (1 bar) sweet chocolate
- 1 slice fresh white bread
- 1 large carrot, pared and cut in 1-inch pieces
- 1 cup walnuts
- 5 eggs, separated
- ¾ cup sugar

**Mocha Buttercream Glaze:**
- 2 ounces sweet chocolate
- 1 tablespoon strong coffee (1 tablespoon water with 1 teaspoon instant coffee)
- 3 tablespoons butter
- ¼ cup confectioners' sugar

1. For torte, melt chocolate in a double boiler and cool.
2. Using **steel blade,** separately process bread to fine crumbs, carrot until grated, and walnuts until finely chopped (see page 10 for processing nuts for torte); remove each from bowl and set aside. Reserve 2 tablespoons of chopped nuts to decorate cake.
3. Still using **steel blade,** process egg yolks with ½ cup sugar until pale and creamy. Add chocolate, stopping to scrape down sides, and process until thoroughly blended.
4. Add bread crumbs and grated carrot and walnuts; process, with quick on/off motions, until thoroughly blended.
5. Using a mixer, beat egg whites with ¼ cup sugar until stiff. Add chocolate mixture and fold together.
6. Pour into a buttered and floured 8-inch springform pan.
7. Bake at 350°F 1¼ hours. Cool before removing from pan.
8. For glaze, melt chocolate with coffee in a double boiler and cool. Using **plastic blade,** process butter. Add chocolate mixture and sugar and process until creamy.
9. Cover top and sides of cake with glaze and sprinkle remaining chopped walnuts over top of cake. Chill until glaze is firm.

*One 8-inch torte*

# Apple Custard Tart

**Crust:**
- 1½ cups flour
- 1½ tablespoons sugar
- ¼ teaspoon salt
- 6 tablespoons frozen butter, cut in 5 pieces
- 2½ tablespoons shortening
- 4½ tablespoons ice water

**Filling:**
- 1½ pounds apples, pared, quartered, and cored
- ½ cup sugar
- 1 teaspoon cinnamon
- ½ teaspoon nutmeg
- ½ cup currants

**Custard:**
- 3 eggs
- ½ cup sugar
- 1 cup whipping cream
- 1 tablespoon vanilla extract
- ¼ cup flour

1. For crust, using **steel blade,** put flour, sugar, salt, frozen butter, and shortening in the bowl; process until crumbly.
2. With machine on, add ice water through feed tube and process until dough forms into a ball.
3. Roll out dough and line a 10-inch quiche pan, pressing dough lightly into bottom of pan. To reinforce the sides, gently lift the edges of the dough and work it down the inside edge of the pan so as to make the sides thicker. Trim off excess dough by passing a rolling pin over the top of the pan.
4. With your thumbs, push the dough ⅛ inch above the edge of the pan. Prick the bottom with a fork. Line with foil or parchment paper and fill with dried beans or rice.
5. Bake at 400°F 10 minutes. Remove foil and beans and cook 8 to 10 minutes longer, or until lightly browned.
6. For filling, using **slicing disc,** slice enough apples to make about 3 cups.
7. Toss apple slices in a bowl with sugar, spices, and currants.
8. Arrange in partially baked shell; turn oven control to 375°F and bake 20 minutes, or until apples are almost tender.
9. Meanwhile, for custard, using **plastic blade,** beat eggs and sugar together until mixture is thick and pale yellow.
10. Add cream and vanilla extract and process. Add flour last and mix until blended and smooth.
11. Push apples gently down into tart and pour custard over top. Bake 30 minutes longer, or until puffy. Sprinkle with **confectioners' sugar** and serve warm.

# Mexican Peach Pastries

**Filling:**
- 1 package (11 ounces) dried peaches
- 1 cup water
- ½ cup sugar
- ½ teaspoon vanilla extract

**Crust:**
- 2 cups flour
- ¾ teaspoon salt
- ½ teaspoon baking powder
- ⅔ cup lard
- 6 tablespoons ice water
  Confectioners' sugar

1. For filling, put peaches and water into a saucepan. Cover, bring to boiling, and cook 20 minutes.
2. Using **steel blade,** add contents of saucepan to bowl and process until pureed.
3. Combine peach puree and sugar in saucepan and cook until thick (about 5 minutes). Cool slightly and stir in vanilla extract. Set aside.

4. For crust, with **steel blade** in bowl, add flour, salt, baking powder, and lard. Process until lard is cut into flour. With machine on, add ice water through feed tube and process until mixture forms into a ball.
5. Divide dough in half. For bottom crust, roll dough to a 15×11-inch rectangle on a lightly floured surface. Fit pastry into a 13×9×2-inch baking pan, pressing gently against bottom and sides of pan. Spread peach mixture evenly over the dough. Roll top crust into a 13×9-inch rectangle and place on top. Fold bottom pastry over onto top. Prick top crust.
6. Bake at 400°F 30 minutes, or until lightly browned around the edges.
7. Cool slightly. Sprinkle with confectioners' sugar. Cut into small squares.

*2 dozen pastries*

# Raspberry Mousse

- 5 packages (10 ounces each) frozen raspberries
- 2 packages unflavored gelatin
- 2 tablespoons lemon juice
- 5 whole eggs
- 4 egg yolks
- ½ cup sugar
- 3 tablespoons raspberry liqueur (optional)
- 2½ cups whipping cream
- 2 tablespoons confectioners' sugar

1. Drain raspberries, reserving juice. Using **steel blade,** process raspberries until pureed. Strain to remove seeds. Discard seeds and set puree adiseset puree aside.
2. In a saucepan, combine lemon juice and 6 tablespoons of reserved raspberry juice. Add gelatin and stir to soften. Stir over low heat until gelatin is dissolved. Let cool.
3. Using **steel blade,** add 5 whole eggs, 4 egg yolks, and sugar to bowl. Process for about 4 to 5 minutes, until very thick. Add raspberry puree and process until combined.
4. With machine on, add cooled gelatin mixture through the feed tube. Process until thoroughly blended. Add raspberry liqueur, if desired.
5. Using a mixer, beat whipping cream until it begins to thicken. Add confectioners' sugar and continue to beat until it holds its shape. Remove one quarter of the whipped cream and save it to decorate the finished mousse.
6. Gently fold whipped cream and raspberry mixture together. Turn into a decorative crystal bowl.
7. Chill mousse until set, at least 2 hours, and decorate with remaining whipped cream put through a pastry bag.

*10 to 12 servings*

# Russian Fruit and Nut Pudding

2 slices dry bread (½ cup crumbs)
12 ounces nuts (walnuts or almonds or both)
1 package (12 ounces) dried fruit (peaches, apricots, or mixed)
2½ cups milk
2½ cups whipping cream
¾ cup semolina
½ cup and 1 tablespoon sugar
½ teaspoon salt
½ teaspoon almond extract
1 cup raisins
2 apples (or any fresh fruit), pared, quartered, and cored
  Lemon juice

1. Using **steel blade,** separately process bread to fine crumbs, nuts until coarsely chopped, and dried fruit until coarsely chopped and remove from bowl.
2. In a heavy saucepan, bring milk and cream to a boil. Stir in semolina and cook about 5 minutes until mixture thickens. Remove from heat and add ½ cup sugar, salt, almond extract, raisins, and chopped dried fruit and mix until thoroughly blended.
3. Using **slicing disc,** slice apples and sprinkle with lemon juice.
4. In a 2-quart casserole, layer a third of semolina mixture. Place half of apple slices on top, then sprinkle with half of chopped nuts. Repeat with a third of semolina mixture, add remaining apple slices and chopped nuts. Top with last third of semolina mixture.
5. Mix bread crumbs with remaining 1 tablespoon sugar and sprinkle over the top of pudding.
6. Bake at 350°F about 30 minutes.
7. Serve warm with **cream.**

*10 to 12 servings*

# Sarah's Lemon Chiffon Pie

**Crust:**
15 graham crackers, broken in quarters
6 tablespoons butter, cut in 6 pieces
¼ cup sugar

**Filling:**
1 envelope unflavored gelatin
¼ cup cold water
3 eggs, separated
¾ cup sugar
½ cup milk
8 ounces cottage cheese
4 ounces cream cheese, cut in pieces
1 teaspoon grated lemon peel
⅓ cup lemon juice
1 teaspoon vanilla extract
¼ teaspoon salt

1. For crust, using **steel blade,** process graham crackers to fine crumbs. Add butter and sugar and process until thoroughly blended. Reserve 2 tablespoons crumbs for topping.
2. Press into a 9-inch glass pie plate.
3. Bake at 375°F about 8 minutes.
4. For filling, soften gelatin in cold water and set aside.
5. Using **steel blade,** process egg yolks and ½ cup sugar until thick and creamy. With machine on, add milk through feed tube and process until mixed.
6. Cook egg mixture in a double boiler over boiling water until it is thickened and coats a spoon. Add gelatin to mixture, stir thoroughly, and set aside to cool.
7. Using **steel blade,** process cottage cheese and cream cheese for a few minutes until smooth. Add lemon peel, lemon juice, vanilla extract, and salt; process until mixed. Add cooled egg-gelatin mixture and process until thoroughly blended.
8. Using a mixer, beat egg whites until frothy. Gradually add ¼ cup sugar and beat until stiff peaks are formed. Add cheese mixture to egg whites and gently fold together.
9. Turn into baked pie shell and chill. Once the pie starts to set, sprinkle remaining crumbs over top of pie. Chill until firm.

*One 9-inch pie*

# INDEX